ASSISTED PASSAGE

WALKING TO FREEDOM
ITALY 1943

To

The many *contadini* without whose bravery, hospitality and help this journey would not have been possible.

Contents

Foreword	9
Preface	11
Disaster at the Wadi Zigzaou	13
Captured	19
Capua and Fontanellato	25
The Armistice and our exit from the Camp	39
We look to the Hills	45
The March—Pessola to Perreto	55
The March—Perreto to Corvara	69
Marking time	93
In the Shadow of the Maiella	105
Through the Lines	123
Epilogue	137
Postscript	139

ASSISTED PASSAGE

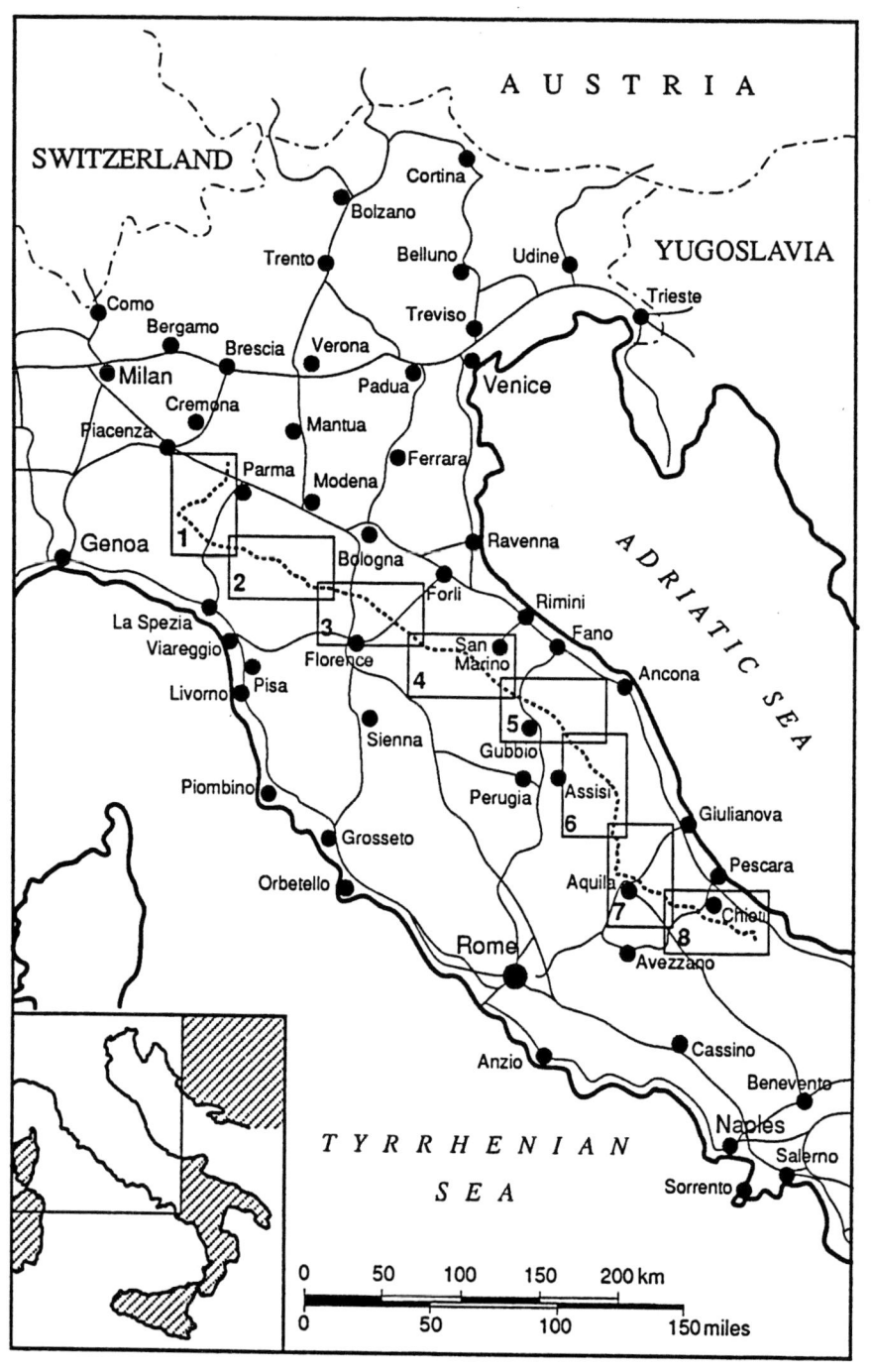

Key to Maps

List of Maps

1 Fontanellato to Vairo, *9 September – 14 October*   38

2 Vairo to Poretta, *14–19 October*   54

3 Poretta to M.Falterona, *19–24 October*   60

4 M.Falterona to Mercatello, *24 October – 2 November*   64

5 Mercatello to Fabriano, *2–6 November*   70

6 Fabriano to Tresungo, *6–12 November*   72

7 Tresungo to Ofena, *12–21 November*   78

8 Ofena to Atessa, *21 November – 23 December*   88

ASSISTED PASSAGE

Plates and Drawings in the Text

The Courtyard and front of the *Orfanotrofio*	Plate 1
Plaque erected by the people of Fontanellato	Plate 1
The first house we came to in Poggio Cancelli	Plate 2
The villages of Calaschio and Rocca Calascio	Plate 2
The village of Corvara	Plate 3
The dam where we crossed the Pescara river	Plate 3
The 'clay screes' which gave us so much trouble on our final walk	Plate 4
Casoli	Plate 4
The rear courtyard of the Orfanotrofio used as the parade ground at Campo PG 49	Page 29
Typical village water pump where we often had a morning wash	Page 59
The street in Poggio Cancelli where Lt. Nicolai lived	Page 81
Sketch of a hut on the slopes of Monte Maiella	Page 117

Foreword

by
Brigadier P. J. Jeffreys, D.S.O., O.B.E..

THIS is a marvellous story told clearly and simply by a fine soldier. Ian English and I have been contemporaries and friends in the Durham Light Infantry for many years. All his splendidly distinguished service was in the 8th Battalion of our great Regiment. Now he gives this account of his escape from his short time as a prisoner of war after capture in the heroic action at Wadi Zigzaou on the Mareth Line in March 1943.

He was then moved from the North African battle field to a prisoner of war camp in Italy, and the major part of his story starts with the Italian Armistice. This gave Ian and many others the opportunity to escape into the Italian countryside. The difficulties then were immense. He had to decide first the size and composition of the party he should try to organise; and then the route they should take. Should they try to get to Switzerland? Should they go towards the advancing British forces three or four hundred miles to the south, and so through the retreating Germans? Or they could stay still, enduring a long wait, till the British forces came up to them?

The problems of finding food, shelter and clothing were formidable. How would the Italian population treat them? Betrayal to the Germans must always be a possibility. In the event the Italian hill farmers bravely gave them and many other Allied servicemen food and shelter.

ASSISTED PASSAGE

This great story tells how these difficulties were met and successfully solved; culminating in a hazardous journey at night through the German lines.

After the end of the adventures described in this book Ian gave himself little rest, for he quickly arranged his own return to duty in his beloved 8th Battalion of the DLI, which fairly soon would be in the lead in D Day's landing in Normandy.

Preface

DURING the journey described in this book, I was able to make cryptic notes about dates, places and people, without mentioning their names of course. When we reached Algiers in January 1944, I visited the map store at Allied Force headquarters and obtained maps covering the whole journey. Armed with these and my notes, during the next three months I wrote a detailed Diary of every day from the 8th September to the 23rd December 1943. Nothing was done with this until 1991 when the urgings of my family and one or two Durham Light Infantry colleagues became too strong to resist. So I decided to write an account from when I was captured to the end of our journey in a rather more 'digestible' form. Without the Diary it would have been nearly impossible.

The whole distance was 500 miles, which I suppose is a long way and it certainly seemed so at the time. But many escapes have covered greater distances than this. It was not as long as that covered by five other ex-inmates of Campo PG 49 at Fontanellato. It was rather shorter than the journeys done by Drew Bethel and Douglas Flowerdew told in the latter's book *Finding the Way*. Or as long as the walk by Tony Davies, Michael Gilbert and Toby Graham described in Tony Davies's enthralling book *When the Moon Rises*. It was a mere Sunday afternoon stroll compared to the journey from Siberia to India by Slavomir Rawicz and his six companions, told in that unforgettable book *The Long Walk*.

This book would probably never have been written without the support, encouragement and sensible suggestions of my wife Lise. Our visit to Italy in September 1992 was largely made possible by my daughter Christine offering to do the driving. She steered us safely through the worst of the eccentric Italian traffic, while I could study the maps and look at the country. These two deserve my sincere thanks. My special thanks to Wilfred 'Scotty' White who jogged my fading memory, particularly of the times not covered by the Diary. Similarly I would like to thank Dennis Neale for the first drawing of the maps and Jim Balmer for his painstaking work to put them in a form suitable for the book. Also Knighton Butterworth for doing the pen and ink sketches which illustrate some of the chapters.

I am especially grateful to Brigadier Peter Jeffreys for contributing the Foreword.

But when all is said and done, it is the many people to whom this book is dedicated, the *contadini*, the peasant farmers of the hills, who I owe the largest debt of gratitude. They took us in when we needed shelter, let us dry our clothes when we were soaked to the skin, they fed us when we were hungry and gave us somewhere to sleep, even if often it was only a draughty barn. In many cases they were poor people, scratching a living from their infertile soils. They helped us and many hundreds of other Allied ex-prisoners of war, in the full knowledge of the consequences if the Germans discovered what they were doing or if they were betrayed by a Fascist-minded fellow countryman. They deserved better recompense from the British authorities than they received.

Disaster at the Wadi Zigzaou

AS the early light of dawn appeared over our right shoulders lighting up the waters of the Wadi Zigzaou, it confirmed my impression that we were in a hopeless defensive position. It was the 23rd March 1943.

It seemed like an age since the battle had started; yet it was only three days since 50 (Northumbrian) Division had launched a frontal attack against the Mareth Line on the night of 20th March. The Line had been termed the 'African Maginot.' The French-built fortifications had previously been considered impregnable, particularly when they were strengthened by minefields. The defences consisted of a series of forts along the north bank of the Wadi Zigzaou, each containing six pill boxes. These were surrounded by a maze of trenches and tunnels. The obstacle was increased by the construction of an anti-tank ditch 12 feet deep and 15 feet wide and the laying of minefields on both sides of the wadi.

The attack by the 151 (Durham) Brigade supported by enormous artillery fire had been successful, and the objectives of the 8th and 9th Battalions of the Durham Light Infantry had been captured, though the enemy resistance in some of the forts had not been completely overcome.

The problem, which reared its ugly head even on the first night, was the building of a crossing of the wadi strong enough to take tanks and wheeled vehicles. The engineers struggled to build this under constant shelling and only four tanks of 50 Royal Tank Regiment got across before dawn. Once daylight came the shelling and sniping of the crossing intensified and continued all day.

We were not threatened during that day, and we watched an Italian counter-attack being effectively dealt with by all thirty-six guns of the 74 Field Regiment RA. But hardly any supplies and certainly no supporting arms particularly anti-tank guns got through to us.

The bridgehead was enlarged on the second night by a successful attack by 6 D.L.I. and 5 East Yorks. After valiant efforts during which they suffered heavy casualties, 50 Division Engineers built a makeshift causeway of fascines. Across this struggled the remainder of 50 R.T.R. But in doing so, they so damaged the causeway that it became impassable for wheeled vehicles or even for carriers. So no anti-tank guns could be got into the bridgehead.

The morning of the second day dawned fine and clear. It was obvious that things were easier, at least for the moment. One could move about with more safety, and I was able to walk over to 6 D.L.I. HQ to talk about the situation with Lt. Colonel Watson and his adjutant Derek Thomlinson. Also we heard and saw the Valentine tanks attempting to move up, though they were soon held up by minefields and anti-tank fire.

About midday we got a message that air reconnaissance had spotted a concentration of about 75 tanks and many infantry in the Zaret area. This was 15 Panzer Division, reinforced, as we learnt later, by a Regiment of 90 Light Division and Ramke Brigade paratroops. Therefore we could soon expect a heavy counter-attack. The order was passed down from the Brigade commander that in the absence of anti-tank guns, the fire of all other weapons must be brought to bear on the tanks.

During the morning there was a very heavy shower and we all got soaked. This dampened our spirits, but something far more serious had happened. The rain had turned the landing grounds into a muddy mess, preventing our fighter bombers taking off. They would have been useful against the forthcoming counter-attack. Also the rain had swollen the water of the Wadi Zigzaou, so that any further crossing of vehicles over the fascine causeway had to be abandoned.

About 1.30 p.m. enemy shelling which had been going on intermittently on the crossing place all morning, increased in intensity, with heavy artillery on the wadi and concentrations of lighter guns on the battalion positions.

The German counter-attack began in earnest about 2.00 p.m. Their first target was the tanks of 50 R.T.R. Their 75 mm and 88 mm guns opened fire at long range and soon knocked out several Valentines which, apart from one tank per troop, were still armed only with the outdated 2 pdr gun. 50 R.T.R. fought a gallant action that afternoon, but were simply outgunned. They lost 30 out of 42 tanks, suffering a lot of casualties including their Commanding Officer Lt. Colonel Cairns.

After about three quarters of an hour three German tanks, two Mark IV Specials (with the 75 mm gun) and a Mark III, loomed up in my C Company area but remained out of grenade range. Presently they came closer and a 68 grenade from 15 Platoon damaged the track of the Mark III. The Germans swept the whole area with long bursts from their tank machine guns, and it was a brave man who raised his head above the parapet sufficiently to fire his rifle or Bren gun.

The only counter measure I could think of was a call to bring down artillery fire on the tanks and the German infantry sheltering behind them. But they were so close that our own positions would be enveloped by fire in the process. However we were well dug in and I reckoned the risk was worth taking. Our artillery fire arrived soon afterwards, and it was a nerve shattering experience, with our own shelling bursting all around our slit trenches. But the Germans must have thought so too, as the tanks pulled back about two hundred yards.

Time wore on and still the Germans had made no direct assault on the company positions, other than heavy shelling and the long terrifying bursts from their tank machine guns.

ASSISTED PASSAGE

Lt. 'Busty' Roberts commander of 15 Platoon sent a runner over to company HQ with a message that he had fifteen wounded men in his platoon, and could something be done for them? I replied 'Not in the presence of these tanks.' Just then another burst of machine gun fire killed the runner. He had joined the company very recently and I never knew his name.

About 5.00 p.m. the enemy shelling increased once more and the tanks came forward firing their machine guns as they advanced. Behind them came some thirty Panzer Grenadiers. We could deal with them with our Brens and rifles, but were prevented from engaging them by the terrible fire of the tank machine guns. One of the tanks came up to 14 Platoon's positions and started to systematically grind in the slit trenches with their tracks. L/Sergeant Holben and eight men, who were all that was left of 14 Platoon, then surrendered. Thereupon Sgt Major Ranson and a Bren gunner from 13 Platoon opened fire at the heads of the tank commanders which made them duck down inside the turrets. It also frightened the German infantry. The tanks replied by firing their 75 mm guns straight at our slit trenches from almost point blank range. Shortly after this Sgt Major Ranson, who was in the next slit trench to me, was carefully raising his Bren gun to the aim when he received a burst of machine gun fire straight through the forehead. So died a very gallant man.

It was now beginning to grow dark, and I thought if only we could hang on till night came we might stand a chance. On the other hand it was obvious that the Germans could take this position if they put in a determined assault by their infantry covered by their tanks. Instead they started shouting to us to surrender, saying our position was hopeless.

B Company appeared to have gone off the air and C Company seemed to be the only unit in touch with Battalion HQ. So I was able to give a running commentary on the course of the battle. But not for much longer. A German tank with infantry riding on it came almost to the road about twelve yards from our positions. Pte Lewis, who had taken over the company HQ Bren gun after Sgt Major Ranson was killed, fired at the infantry and we hurled 36 grenades at them. The infantry immediately sheared off and presently the tanks did also. The commander evidently called for more artillery support, because soon afterwards a really vicious 'stonk' came down on the company positions. A shell landed between my trench and that of L/Corporal Simpson, who up till then had been operating the RT set as calmly as if he was on an exercise. The shell blew the No. 18 set about three feet in the air. So now we too were out of contact with Battalion HQ. The only ammunition remaining in the company was .303 for the rifles and Brens and there was not much of that. It seemed the end could not be long delayed. It was now almost 7.00 p.m. and darkness had fallen; and the Germans seemed to have pulled back a little.

Then out of the darkness behind us came a man running with a message from Battalion HQ. It told us to withdraw to the anti-tank ditch. There was no time for questions, the man was gone almost as soon as he came.

I got a message to 13 and 15 Platoons, telling them to pull out bringing as many wounded and as many weapons as they could. Some of the wounded were brought back, but unfortunately quite a number had to be left to be taken prisoner. The company collected in low ground behind our old positions. We numbered three officers and twenty three men. At midday we had totalled sixty including three officers.

At the anti-tank ditch I was met by Major Bob Lidwill, who had been brought up from the rear to take over command after Lt. Colonel Jackson had been killed and the second in command Major Blackden wounded. He put C Company on the left of the battalion joining up with Captain George Wood's company of 6 D.L.I. We dug trenches in the top of the anti-tank ditch. What was left of the brigade was in a long thin line along the ditch, a very precarious position.

ASSISTED PASSAGE

Everyone was dog tired having been in action for three nights and two days. All we wanted to do was sleep. But sentries had to be posted; and it was essential that rifles, Brens and Tommy guns were cleaned as many of the working parts were clogged with sand. We were warned that we would have to launch a new attack on Ouerzi, the fort which was the original objective of A and B Companies. But the idea seemed so unrealistic that I did not worry about it.

Then came the dawn.

Captured

WHEN it became fully light I felt it necessary to liaise with the company on my right to tie up defensive fire tasks. There had been no opportunity the previous night as we occupied the position in the dark.

So I told my company headquarters where I was going and set off down the anti-tank ditch. Having gone about a hundred yards I was surprised to find no soldiers about at all. So I went further on thinking they must have been moved to the right. There was a bend in the ditch near the point where it had been filled in by the Sappers to make a roadway. I walked round this bend and ran into five German Panzer Grenadiers at about twenty yards distance. I suppose I should have turned and run off back down the anti-tank ditch. Instead, we looked at each other for a moment, then I pulled out my revolver and fired six shots. I have never been a good shot with a revolver, and in a state of shock and considerable fatigue, all I succeeded in doing was to hit one of the Germans in the foot. One of them fired a shot which went over my head. When I had emptied the magazine of the revolver I threw it on the ground, and stood looking at the Germans with my hands on my hips. I did not want to put them in the air. They then came and searched me for more weapons and arrested me.

I then realised I had been extremely fortunate not to have been shot out of hand. That was the second time in this battle that my Guardian Angel had been watching over me. The first was in the original attack when I felt something hit my chest, but did not take much notice at the time. Later when things were quieter, I saw there was a slit in the left hand breast pocket of my battle dress blouse. In the pocket was a bullet which had hit the crucifix given to me early in the war by my mother and which had been blessed by a Father Costello.

I was led off through the anti-tank ditch and up the hill towards our old positions. It was perhaps the most depressing walk of my life. Apart from the realisation that I was a prisoner in the hands of the enemy, we were walking over the ground on which the battle had been fought for the last three days.

I first noticed the Valentine tanks of 50 R.T.R. Some were lying at all angles with jagged holes in their armour. Others were on fire with small arms ammunition exploding inside them. Several fires created a pall of smoke over the whole area. In and around the forts which the D.L.I. companies had captured and occupied was the whole detritus of war. Dead German, Italian and British soldiers lay on the ground or slumped in the trenches. Rifles, machine guns and other weapons lay about and pieces of equipment, mess tins, ammunition boxes, magazines and steel helmets were scattered everywhere. It was indescribable confusion and chaos. Over everything was the all-pervading stench of death and destruction.

Eventually to my great relief we came out of the battle area, and I was marched over open, undulating ground towards Zaret. Here were a few buildings and palm trees.

I was taken to a group of tents which was obviously a headquarters of some sort. After waiting some time, I was taken into a tent and questioned by a German officer who spoke excellent English, and who was very correct and polite. Having given my name, rank and number as one is obliged to do, he looked at my shoulder flashes and recognised that I was in 8 D.L.I., which he knew of course was in 50 Division. He asked about my background and parents, and how long I had been in the army. He knew where 50 Division had been during the war, and asked if I had been with them all the time. He got no answers to these questions. He talked about Rommel, saying he was a sick man and he had now gone home to Germany to recuperate. That was certainly news to me.

Then he shot a question at me: 'What are these Scorpions?' (Scorpion was the code name of a recently introduced flail tank which had chains mounted on extended arms at the front. These chains thrashed the ground to explode mines, and so clear a path through minefields). I said 'I don't know, I've never heard of them.' With that I was dismissed.

I was taken outside and presently saw Sgt Morgan the platoon sergeant of 13 platoon in C Company. He had just been interrogated. He was amazed how much the Germans knew about us including the name of the Commanding Officer—Lt. Colonel Jackson. They drop pieces of information into the conversation to make the prisoner think they know everything, and therefore there is no harm in telling them what you know. Sgt Morgan had been captured when we withdrew from our positions last evening. We had a short chat but were then separated.

I now had two contrary emotions. First was one almost of relief. The physical danger was over or at any rate considerably reduced, and the weight of responsibility as a company commander taken off me. On the other hand I knew I should be looking for opportunities to escape. It is well known that it is easier to escape soon after capture than it is later on. But so far the Germans had made sure there was no nonsense of that sort. On the march from the Mareth Line I had a German soldier with a Schmeisser sub-machine gun close behind me, and now another who appeared equally attentive had taken over.

After some time I was taken to join a group of about twenty five other prisoners, several of whom were D.L.I. One of these was a fair-haired young lieutenant called Scotty White. He had been in Major Teddy Worrall's company of 9 D.L.I., and on the first day of the battle we had met for a few minutes in the sunken road which ran between our two positions. Now he was hobbling about as he had been wounded in the foot.

Later that day we were bundled into trucks and taken north to Sfax, which is on the railway line between Tunis and Gabes.

ASSISTED PASSAGE

The next day, 24th March, the whole party which now numbered about a hundred was put into cattle trucks, with about thirty five in each truck, and the doors barred and bolted. We now started a very slow journey with many stops for unexplained reasons. We were very crowded in the truck, and there was not room for everyone to lie down at once. Scotty White managed to do so which was just as well with his wounded foot. There were a few short stops when we were allowed out to relieve ourselves, and once a day we were given some dark bread and a drink of weak coffee.

We reached Sousse on 25th March. The next day there was a very long stop, and the Germans opened the doors. As it was in the middle of open country we asked one of the guards the cause of the stop. He replied *'ligne kaput,'* from which we deduced that the railway line had been cut by Allied bombing.

We eventually reached Tunis, our destination, on 26th March. After a lot of hanging about, we were marched some way to a long low group of buildings, which we were told had been a tyre factory. Here were about three to four hundred British prisoners, the great majority from 1st Army. There seemed to be many Grenadier and Coldstream Guards officers who had been captured in an unsuccessful battle near Medjez el Bab. Two of these were Mark Bonham Carter and Lord Brabourne.

The Germans had made an agreement with the Italians that Allied prisoners taken in North Africa would be handed over to the Italians, once they had left the battle area. I know that many British prisoners would have preferred to remain in German hands; not because they were kinder to them, but because their administration was more efficient which made living conditions more tolerable. This was certainly true of those captured in the summer of 1942, who suffered disease and distress due to poor or nonexistent sanitary arrangements provided by the Italians.

So at this point our German escorts handed us over to the Italians who ran the transit camp in the rubber factory. Of course this meant we would eventually be taken to prison camps in Italy, not in Germany.

The days in the tyre factory were uneventful and tedious in the extreme, and one day merged into another. Meals were insufficient and tasteless, but I suppose were what one could expect in a prison camp. However these days did enable me to get to know Scotty White. A point in common was that we had both been at King's College, Newcastle before the war. He was reading Zoology, whereas I had done one year of the Agriculture course. He stayed on after the war started to complete his degree. He then joined the Ministry of Agriculture in the Entomology Department. His work was concerned with pests, particularly wireworm which were a problem in crops following old grassland, which was being ploughed up to grow arable feed crops. He had to visit farms to take samples and give advice and also carry out the laboratory assessments. But he became disenchanted with the work and sought a more active role in the war effort. So he resigned and joined the Army, being posted to the Border Regiment. His unit was being trained as glider pilots. Having no desire to fly a glider into battle, he applied for service abroad and joined a party of reinforcements for the Middle East. So it was that he was posted to 9 D.L.I. in August or September 1942. He was wounded in his first action, in the Operation Supercharge attack during the battle of El Alamein and spent the next three months in hospital. Being keen to get back to 9 D.L.I., he was able to rejoin them when the brigade was at Benina near Benghazi.

Scotty was an equable character who took everything as it comes. He did not easily get in a 'flap' which was to prove a benefit later on. We hit it off together from the first days.

One evening someone organised an impromptu singsong, and there were some good turns. It is surprising the talent one finds on occasions of this sort. Even Scotty and I were persuaded to get up and sing 'Blaydon Races.'

We noticed that a road ran along the side of the factory and across this was an orchard which seemed to afford quite good cover. Scotty suggested that if we could open a large steel door, we might be able to make a quick dash across the road to the orchard and get away. One evening we managed to get the door open a few inches, wide enough we thought to squeeze through. But the Italians were well aware of the danger and had a sentry covering the door. So that put a stop to our only, and ineffectual, escape attempt from this camp.

Two days later on the 5th April we were moved to the docks in Tunis. The Italians were anxious to get all their prisoners over to Italy as soon as possible. They could see that sooner or later the Allies would probably capture Tunis, which would result in us being freed. We were put aboard a merchant ship. As we were going down to the hold we watched about twenty large three-engined German transport planes flying in only a few feet above the sea. No doubt this was to avoid being intercepted and shot up by Allied fighters. The Germans were obviously reinforcing Tunisia as hard as they could.

Between four and five hundred prisoners were crowded into the hold and the hatches battened down. Twice a day one hatch was opened and we were allowed to go up the gangway one at a time to the latrine.

We lay in Tunis harbour for about a day and a half before sailing. We knew that the Royal Navy and the R.A.F. had been sinking a large tonnage of Axis shipping in the narrow waters between Tunis and Italy. So naturally we were very anxious about the crossing. Our fears were increased when we observed that many of the crew and the guards had their boots either undone or round their necks, and had their life jackets on. We did not rate our chances very highly of getting out of that crowded hold if the ship was attacked. Therefore it was with considerable relief that we docked at Naples on 8th April.

Capua and Fontanellato

AFTER we disembarked we were kept in the dock area for some time. A few of us got talking to an Italian who was working there. He was rather proud of his fine voice, and willingly sang some pieces from various operas. This helped the waiting time to pass. A short train journey and then we marched into the prisoner of war camp at Capua.

The camp, numbered PG 66, was designed as a prisoner of war transit camp, and normally one would not be there for more than a month or two before being moved to one of the permanent camps. However we were very glad to settle down in one place for a while after the long slow journey first from Mareth to Tunis, and then in the crowded smelly ship across to Naples, and lastly to Capua.

The camp was a series of wooden sheds with tin roofs, each holding about twenty men. There was a mess hut where we ate and held occasional meetings. The fairly primitive ablutions and latrines were off to one side. The camp was made up of a number of compounds, each surrounded by barbed wire in addition to the wire fence which surrounded the whole camp.

It was in Capua that I was introduced to the Red Cross parcel. Here it is appropriate to pay tribute to the wonderful organisation set up by the Red Cross to provide a food parcel on the basis of one per week for every Allied prisoner of war wherever they were. The fact that not every prisoner always received one was not the fault of the Red Cross, but was due to transport or other difficulties in Italy or Germany. In the case of Japan of course it was the policy to have as little contact with the Red Cross as possible, and certainly not to allow the giving of food parcels. Fortunately for prisoners in Europe, the parcels meant the difference between the extremely plain and barely adequate ration provided by the Italians and a very much more interesting and better balanced diet. There must have been a vast organisation behind this. It is not too much to say that the Red Cross saved many prisoners lives during the war. Although it often took some time after a move for the numbers on the 'ration strength' for parcels to be adjusted, leading to delays in issuing parcels to prisoners; we were fortunate in that we received them almost as soon as we got to Capua.

There were two kinds of Red Cross parcel—British and Canadian. The latter was slightly more popular because it seemed to have greater variety. For instance they contained a tin of spam which was quite a favourite. The main difference was that the English parcel contained a tin of condensed milk; whereas the Canadian had a tin of dried whole milk powder named Klim. If one was feeling extravagant one could make a liquid resembling cream by adding more powder. Also the empty tins were very useful for making all sorts of things. Otherwise both parcels provided a tin of stew, meat loaf, creamed rice, sardines or pilchards, a bar of chocolate and ten cigarettes.

At Capua we did our own cooking; either individually or three or four joining together to make a better meal. The food provided by the Italians was reasonable, I suppose, by prison camp standards. There was never enough of it, but what was there was eatable. The coffee was almost undrinkable. We were nearly always hungry. Cooking for ourselves usually meant keeping opened tins of food under our beds which was far from hygienic. We were never allowed to have unopened tins as this might have been an aid to escaping.

We passed the time by chatting in groups, or going for endless walks round and round the small compound, or by merely lying on our beds dozing. Some officers offered to give talks about all sorts of subjects. I remember two in particular. One by a big strapping lad was on his experiences working on

Norwegian whalers. He vividly described the hard life aboard these ships in the Antarctic seas. He worked both on factory ships and the smaller boats carrying the harpoons. The only reason men went to sea on these vessels was the money which was very good. Otherwise the life was disagreeable in the extreme. Long hours and heavy work often in Antarctic gales and over everything was the overpowering stench of the whale carcases and blubber.

The second talk was given by Lt. Colonel Everitt who had been the commanding officer of a battalion of the Kings Own Regiment. I had first met him when he was the Regular Adjutant of 8 D.L.I. when I applied to join in 1938. He left late in that year handing over to Andrew Clarke. Colonel Everitt's battalion had been flown in to Habbaniya at very short notice at the time of the Iraqi insurrection in May 1941. It was mainly due to the prompt and resolute action of his battalion which prevented the Iraqis capturing this important air base. He made the whole thing sound most amusing which belied the skilful handling of the operation.

I developed a nasty abscess on my left cheek. I had no wish to consult an Italian doctor, as their medical service had a very bad reputation among the British doctors. Fortunately a fellow prisoner was Captain Webster who had been medical officer of the 7th Green Howards, and who I had got to know when I was attached to them in August 1940. He produced a scalpel from somewhere and lanced the abscess, which I am glad to say healed up soon afterwards.

Having been a month at Capua we were told to get ready for a move. On 11th May we were entrained in cattle trucks and did an overnight journey to the north. In the evening the train stopped in some large marshalling yards. We were allowed out of the trucks to relieve the call of nature and we asked where we were. The guard said *'Roma.'* I thought this was perhaps not the best way to see the glorious city of Rome, but at least we could say we had been there. On the morning of 12th May we arrived at Fidenza in the Plain of Lombardy.

Here we were put in trucks and driven through the flat fertile countryside of the Po valley known as the *Pianura Padana*, to the village of Fontanellato, about twelve and a half miles north west of Parma.

PG 49, as this prisoner of war camp was known, was on the edge of the village of Fontanellato. It was a large modern building with a classical façade, with three floors and a basement connected by a marble staircase; and it had two wings one on each side of a large central hall.

It had been built as an orphanage, but when the war came it had remained empty, until the Italian authorities decided early in 1943 to use it as a camp for Allied officer prisoners. We slept in dormitories of various sizes. I was in a large room on the third floor holding about twenty beds, and there were smaller rooms with six to ten beds. They were beds, not double tiered bunks common to many camps. Beside each bed was a small cupboard for personal belongings. There were wash basins and lavatories on each floor, with showers in the basement. So we were really very comfortable, though perhaps rather crowded. In the camp were about four hundred officer prisoners and about a hundred other ranks who did the cooking and other administrative work. All in all Fontanellato must have been one of the best prisoner of war camps in Italy.

One major change from Capua for the better was that all the cooking was done centrally, and we never saw our Red Cross parcels. A messing committee arranged the menus, integrating the parcel food with the Italian rations. The result was we ate pretty well, and as we went down to the basement for our meals we were fairly sure we would be offered something good. In addition to this the officers running the administration took over the cigarette ration from the parcels. Those who smoked could buy cigarettes using camp lira, but the rest were used to buy food and some drink from outside on the very active black market.

Another advantage of this camp was that all the laundry was done by nuns who lived in a convent next door to the orphanage. I am not sure how this was paid for, but the results were excellent. Some prisoners put soap in with their laundry, and they would get back little notes saying the sisters were praying for them.

Adjoining the convent was the *sanctuario*, the shrine of the miraculous *Madonna del Rosario*. Once or twice each day its bells were rung. Some prisoners welcomed this, as it relieved the monotony of the uneventful days; but it jarred on the nerves of others.

Soon after being taken up to my dormitory on the top floor, in came Tommy Preacher. He had joined 8 D.L.I. in the spring of 1939, and was second in command of D Company

The rear courtyard of the Orfanotrofio used as the parade ground at Campo PG 49

when Rosscol was attacked by German tanks in April 1942 and he was taken prisoner. He said 'Hallo Tubby! By Jove you are not so tubby now.' I had lost a lot of weight after I was wounded on 5th June 1942 and was now rather too thin. Then and later we had long chats about our respective experiences since we had last seen each other. British soldiers captured in the summer of 1942 suffered dreadfully in the prison camps run by the Italians in the desert. The hygiene and sanitary arrangements were so bad that many prisoners got dysentery and some died.

Another two 8 D.L.I. officers were in PG 49. C. J. Woods and E. N. Strickland had been subalterns in D Company with Tommy Preacher, and had been captured in the same operation. A pleasant surprise was to meet Donald Shaw. He had been a school prefect with me at Oundle, and I believe he was Head Boy in the term after I was in 1938. He was the signals officer of a brigade in Tobruk when he was captured.

The majority of my room mates were officers of the 1st Battalion Duke of Cornwall Light Infantry. They had been in 10 Indian Division which had been rushed up to the Tobruk area when the Gazala battles were turning against 8th Army in June 1942. They had been taken prisoner in their first action. One of these was Captain Floyer-Acland, the son of General Floyer-Acland, at that time the Military Secretary. Another was Captain Watson, also the son of a general. The man in the next bed to me was a Lt. Williams, a Gurkha officer. He was very interesting about the life of a British officer in the Gurkhas. At the far end of the dormitory was another Old Oundelian, Jack Gatford. He had been a very good scrum half at school, and then went to Woolwich and became a regular officer in the Royal Engineers. He was involved in a very active bridge school which played bridge endlessly, followed by interminable post-mortems far into the night. He was later to get a rugger blue at Cambridge when he was rather surprisingly chosen at scrum half just before the Varsity match in 1947. Jack Moore was also in my dormitory. He was a quiet well spoken man who had been given an Immediate Commission in the Field and also had been awarded the Military Medal with the Northumberland Hussars. He had a rather fine voice, and used to sing solos in the impromptu concerts which were arranged from time to time. We were to be very closely involved with each other in future months. Scotty White was in the same room as I, but Tommy Preacher slept in a smaller room with some officers of the South Notts. Hussars—the Sherwood Rangers.

The Italian Commandant was a very smart colonel who had a reputation of being fair. He realised it was our duty to try to escape, but he would do everything in his power to prevent us. I heard he had played bridge for Italy before the war. It was sad that he was later arrested by the Germans for conniving at our escape from the camp after the Armistice. His second in command Captain Comino had been in business in London before the war. He was in the Alpini Regiment, and was always dressed in immaculate uniform which included a long feather in his hat. He was often seen going round the camp smoking a pipe looking like an English country gentleman, and he was always friendly towards us. The other interpreter named Prevedini who, though outwardly friendly, was a sly, untrustworthy character. The guards were mainly reservists, small miserable looking men, as tired of their dull life guarding us as we were of being guarded.

We often tried to score points over the Italians. For instance in the afternoon the guard was changed in a ceremony in the courtyard below our windows. Amid much blowing of bugles, the guards fixed bayonets. As they pulled the bayonets out of the scabbards they shouted 'Savoy,' presumably in honour of the king. Each afternoon we anticipated this, and as they shouted 'Savoy' we shouted 'Oy.' After a few days the Italians could stand it no more, and Prevedini and three soldiers came running up to our room and demanded to know who had been shouting and ridiculing the House of Savoy. We received an almighty ticking off, but no one was put in the 'cooler' (solitary confinement). The Senior British Officer (SBO) and others established close relations with the camp staff, and this worked very much in our favour towards the end of our time at Fontanellato.

There were always two roll calls each day; though there could be more if the Italians thought there was something amiss. The procedure was to file past individually the two camp staff who were doing the counting. This often took ages, partly because many officers did not cooperate and treated the whole business in a slack unmilitary manner. When Colonel de Burgh arrived to take over from Lt. Colonel Lowsley Williams as SBO, he sensed that a proportion of the prisoners had forgotten they were serving officers in the British Army. So he ordered a general smartening up and instilled some discipline into us.

One of his measures was to organise the whole camp as if it was an infantry battalion. There were four officer companies and an other ranks company, with a Lt. Colonel in charge of each. The companies were split into three platoons each with a commander. Each company commander had the assistance of an adjutant. I was appointed adjutant of No. 2 company whose commander was Lt. Colonel Everitt whom I mentioned in connection with our time at Capua. The SBO had a small staff. Lt. Colonel Hugh Mainwaring, late headquarters 8th Army, acted as his second in command or chief of staff. Lt. Colonel Wheeler, late GSO1 50 Division, was made responsible for Intelligence. From then on we paraded in our companies for roll calls, and these were completed to the satisfaction of the Italians in very much less time than under the old system.

The morning roll call was followed by breakfast. After that time was our own. It was interesting to see how many different ways the prisoners found to pass the time. Some, more particularly those who had been prisoners for some time, sat about and talked in groups or merely stared out of the window. Others spent the day playing bridge or baccarat.

There were several accomplished painters in the camp and a very good art exhibition was held. There was quite an emphasis on education and several courses on a wide range of subjects were run. For example a few officers studied law, others journalism and there were several language classes. I joined about six others in an agriculture class taken by a big fresh faced Lincolnshire farmer. It was perforce very theoretical, but was enjoyable and worthwhile nonetheless.

These classes and life generally were enhanced by a good camp library. This had been built up by books from other camps and also from the British library in Rome. The sending of books from home was allowed. If they were hardbacks the binding was removed by the authorities in case they contained concealed maps. But many were rebound with cardboard from Red Cross parcels. Officers gave books of fiction to the library after they had finished with them. I did a lot of reading in the camp and found it was a marvellous way to pass the time.

Some people were keen on theatricals, and an excellent drama group was running in which were some experienced actors and producers. One show was a performance of Somerset Maugham's *The Circle*. These performances were always popular because, whatever the standard, they took one out of the atmosphere of the prison camp and a chance to think of other things.

Captain Kane Burman was one of the prisoners. He was a South African dentist. He was able to obtain some instruments from the Italians and set up a treatment room in one of the wings of the orphanage. Assisted by a Canadian doctor, he examined the teeth of all the prisoners. My teeth had got into a bad state, and one afternoon they took several of them out, under pentothol anæsthetic I should add.

The large hall was an ideal place to hold meetings, concerts and sing songs. We were fortunate that among the senior officers was Lt. Colonel Hugh Mainwaring who had been GSO1 (Operations) at 8th Army Headquarters. Immediately after the end of the battle of El Alamein, he had been a little too keen in pushing forward to find a new site for Army headquarters, and was captured by German rearguards near Mersa Matruh. He gave four lectures on the Desert war from the 1940/41 campaign against the Italians, the Crusader operation in November 1941, the fighting at Gazala with the long retreat back to Alamein and finally the Battle of El Alamein itself. Most of the prisoners had perforce a very limited view of the fighting and of the battle as a whole, and probably were captured amid considerable confusion. Mainwaring gave us a broad picture of these battles and was able to explain the reasons for actions which up till then had been something of a mystery. He gave a fascinating account of how he and others developed the J system which, by listening in to the forward radio net of headquarters from brigade to corps, obtained a much clearer knowledge of the state of the battle and the position of our forward troops. They could therefore make the support of the Desert Air Force immeasurably more effective.

Shortly before I arrived at Fontanellato a sports ground immediately beyond the compound had been constructed. The barbed wire fences were extended and sentry boxes erected at each Corner. This was a boon and enabled us to play small team rugger and soccer games, and two basket ball posts were set up. Lt. Gardner a Royal Tank Regiment officer who had played first class basket ball in Canada, instructed some keen participants. A running track was marked out and a variety of races were staged. By the end of the summer very little grass was left on the pitch. The Italian sentries, and the many villagers who watched, were amazed as the 'mad dogs of Englishmen' played seven a side rugger on a bone hard ground in the heat of the afternoon. A knock-out competition was organised. Among the other ranks were a number of South Africans who were good rugger players and who were more accustomed to the hard conditions than were the British officers. I do not think any officers' team managed to beat them. Running down the middle of the sports ground was a small stream. The racing fraternity used to race sticks or corks down the stream and had great excitement betting on the results.

A number of officers made continuing efforts to escape. There was an Escaping Committee which controlled activities, and anyone who thought he had a feasible plan had to put it up to the committee for approval. This avoided clashes between different schemes, and made the best use of resources such as clothing and identity cards. While I was at Fontanellato five officers succeeded in getting out of the camp. Lt. Day and a companion hid in a hole they had dug in the sports ground, concealed from the guards by a mock rugby scrum. When the sports ground was cleared at 5.00 p.m. they remained hidden. The roll call was rigged, and another check round the dormitories by the orderly officer in the early hours showed nothing was amiss. The two got through the wire during the night and travelled for nearly four weeks. But they had the great misfortune to be arrested when they were in sight of the Swiss frontier.

The second attempt was made by Tony Roncoroni, an enormous man who had played rugger for England several times as a second row forward in the thirties, and two companions, got out by the same method three nights later. But the next morning the Italians became suspicious and the alarm was given. The three were brought back within a couple of days.

I took little part in the escaping activity except to do a few turns as lookout when work on the tunnel was being carried out. This was very difficult work and did not get very far, and was finally stopped by the guards digging a trench ten feet deep right round the camp. All we could do was to watch and jeer as the little soldiers sweated at their digging in the hot Italian summer.

A great benefit which we really enjoyed was being allowed out of camp for walks about once a week or ten days. It was clearly understood that we were on parole, nevertheless we were heavily guarded. We turned out smartly dressed in the courtyard and set off at a brisk pace. This was partly to make for more energetic exercise and partly to annoy the Italians. Their small and not very fit reservists soldiers could not keep up, and the three men at the back were soon left far behind, while those at the front were having their heels trodden on by the leading British prisoners. We soon came to know the countryside as we explored the many lanes in the Fontanellato area, as the guards would not take us on to main roads. The amazing fertility of the soil was there for all to see. We passed fields growing splendid crops of wheat, sugar beet and tomatoes. The maize had grown a foot since we had last seen it the week before, and the luscious fields of grapes made our mouths water. Apart from the enjoyment of the exercise these walks gave us a view of the outside world.

At one end of the gallery above the hall a bar was set up. The camp purchasing organisation bought in red wine and vermouth, and we were allowed one glass of each per day. The red wine, termed *vini lavoroti* by the Italians, was sour and I never got to like it, but the vermouth was quite palatable. From the bar window we could see the road outside, and we often stood and watched the villagers going by, while they stared at us. We welcomed Sunday evenings when the village girls turned out in force, and both sides got a vicarious pleasure in staring at each other. These were the first girls most of the prisoners had seen for many months or years in some cases. Perhaps they seemed more attractive by the fact that it was 'forbidden fruit.' Wanda Newby in her book *Peace and War* has described how the girls' official reason for coming past the camp was to pay their respects to a relative's grave in the nearby cemetery. But we noticed that many did not get as far as the inside of the cemetery!

The morale of the prisoners in the camp was generally very high. This was the result of fairly comfortable living conditions, good camp organisation and reasonably accurate news of how the war was progressing. It has to be said that quite a number of prisoners were quite content with their lot and did not want things to change. They knew where their next meal was coming from, they did not have to do anything unless they wanted to, and they had no important decisions to make. A degree of moral turpitude could easily set in.

It was not till later that we realised how fortunate we were compared to the prisoners in many camps in Italy and Germany; or indeed to the ghastly conditions endured by the Russians and Germans in each others' hands, and the Allied prisoners of the Japanese.

A good news service was run by an American journalist who had been on HMS *Ark Royal* when she was sunk in the Mediterranean. He posted on the notice board the official Italian communiqués and extracts from the newspapers. One learnt to read between the lines to find out what was really going on. For example phrases such as 'Our gallant soldiers are writing their names on the pages of history with their blood,' one knew they had probably suffered a heavy defeat.

There was also a clandestine radio set up in the camp, the whereabouts of which was a closely guarded secret. I was told this set had been made entirely in the camp out of Red Cross parcel tins and camp wire. The only exception was the valves which by some devious means were brought in from outside. British broadcasts were listened to on this set, and the American skilfully worked the news received in this way with that printed in the Italian papers, so as to conceal the source of the information. He always started his accounts with the word 'FLASH.' On 21st July we heard a large commotion and cheering in the guard room and in the road outside. Soon afterwards a news Bulletin was posted on the board. It began 'FLASH, Benito finito!' The SBO called a parade in the hall, and told us that Mussolini had been deposed and Marshal Badoglio had taken his place. The Fascist regime was at an end.

ASSISTED PASSAGE

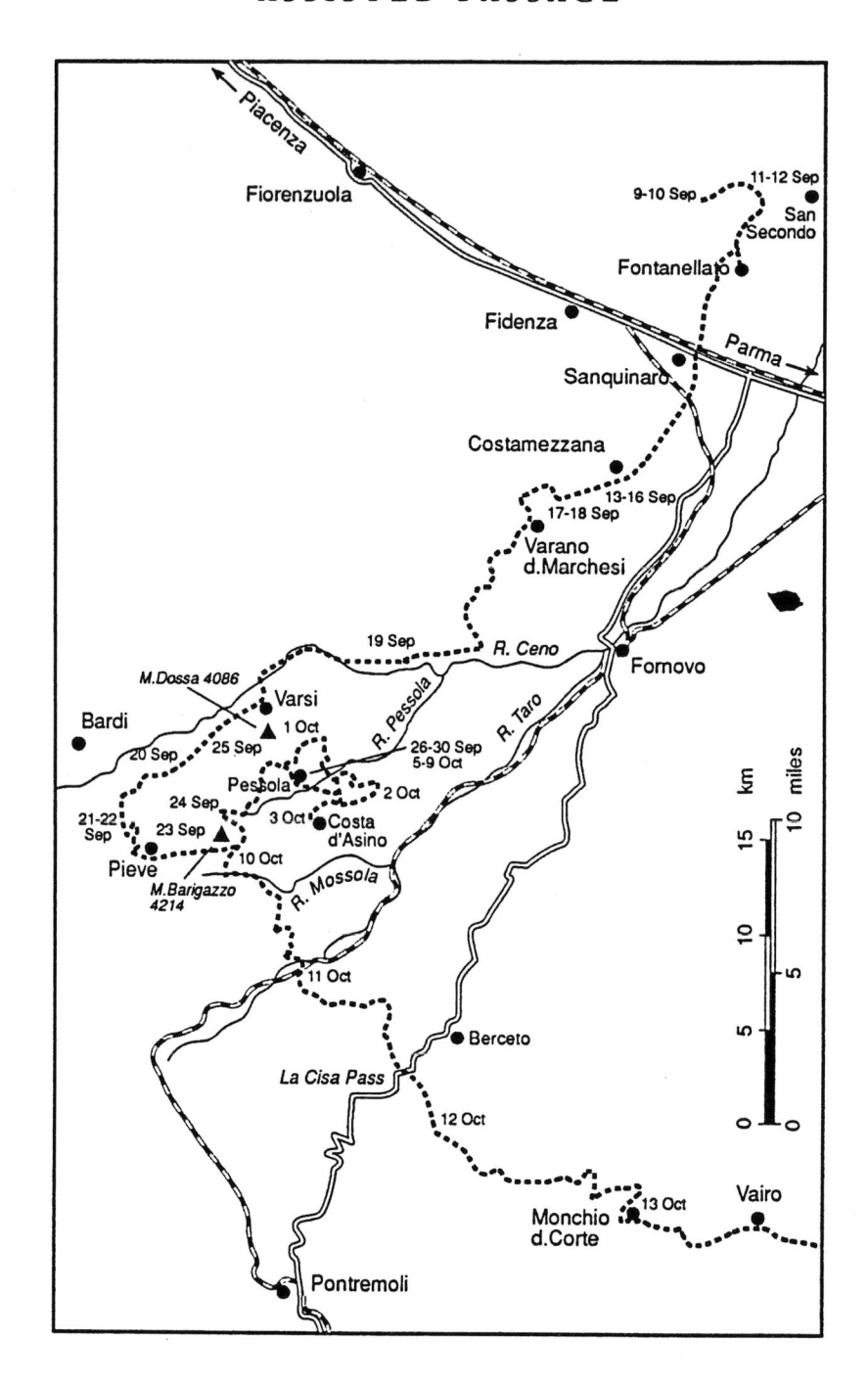

The Armistice and our exit from the Camp

FOLLOWING the overthrow of Mussolini and his government, everyone thought Marshal Badoglio would sign an armistice with the Allies and take Italy out of the war. Some inveterate gamblers took bets that we would be home by Christmas. However nothing happened, which for us was an anti climax.

Now a new anxiety came to the surface. Would the Germans come in and take over the camp? We had long discussions about what their actions would be if Italy surrendered. Several said they would pull back to the line of the river Po or even to the Alps. In hindsight this was not a sensible forecast. Obviously they would strive to keep the Allies as far away from Germany as possible. On one or two occasions we had seen German companies marching past the camp looking very military indeed, carrying rifles and light automatics. We noticed that one man would shout a number and immediately the whole party would start singing the song of that number. Perhaps it was done to impress the allied prisoners of war.

August passed uneventfully. The campaign in Sicily had been successfully concluded. We now saw the benefit of the good relations which the SBO had established with the camp Commandant. The SBO reminded the latter that in the event of an Armistice, it was the Commandant's responsibility to ensure the safety of the prisoners until they could be handed over to the British authorities. The Commandant accepted this

Every SBO had been given a War Office order that in the event of an Armistice, prisoners should remain in their camps until further orders were received. This was thought to be for the safety of the prisoners themselves, as they would be unprotected if they wandered about in the countryside. Fortunately Colonel de Burgh interpreted this order in the light of circumstances in his camp at the time. In other camps, notably Chieti, the order was strictly enforced, resulting in large numbers of prisoners being taken to Germany.

The evening of 8th September was hot and sultry. After supper I was lying on my bed reading, when there was a great commotion amongst the Italian soldiers and the villagers on the road outside. We went to the window to see what was happening. Ernie Brett a D.C.L.I. officer said they were shouting *'pace' 'armisticia.'* I thought he was imagining it as the wish was father to the thought. Certainly there was tremendous excitement in the courtyard below and round the guard room. The soldiers were shouting, dancing round and throwing their caps in the air. Presently the Commandant came over to our building from his office. A few minutes later the word went round to assemble in the main hall. The SBO said he had had an unconfirmed report of an Armistice. Everyone had to remain calm and dignified, and he would try to keep us in touch with the latest news. This was indeed a memorable occasion.

It was later confirmed that an Armistice between the Allies and Italy had been signed, and given off to the world at 7.22 p.m. Also it was rumoured that the Germans were leaving Italy as fast as they could! This was the day we had all been waiting for.

The next morning we noticed that about thirty Italian soldiers were setting up machine guns on the sentry boxes. Then we were ordered to parade outside for instructions. The SBO told us that the Commandant had received information that the Germans were going to attack the camp to recover the prisoners. We were therefore going out into the country, taking haversack rations, to lie up till the situation was clearer. We had to pack, taking just a haversack, and be ready to move at five minutes notice. Rumours abounded and we heard that the Allies had landed at Naples, Livorno, La Spezia and

THE ARMISTICE

Genoa. Even now I and a few others did not think we would go out.

I was busy passing on orders from Colonel Everitt to platoons and sections of the company. But there was time for Scotty White and I to have a drink of vermouth in the bar, which of course was packed. At 12 noon the bugle sounded the alarm call of three 'G's and we paraded with our kit on the playing field. Our No. 2 Company was the first to be collected, and away we went following Lt. Colonel Mainwaring and Captain Comino through a gap cut in the wire. There seemed to be an air raid alert on at the time. It was a great feeling to be crossing fields without attendant guards. The farther we got from the camp the safer we felt. On the way out a Junkers 52 flew over very low, and we thought it must have seen us. We marched out about five miles to a river with high earth banks, well covered by trees which afforded good cover. Colonel Mainwaring, who had reconnoitred the place in the morning, laid out the company areas. We were mainly disposed under vines in fields and along the river side. We had some lunch and brewed tea. The orders were to keep under cover, but to mount sentries for our own protection.

That night was damp and rather cold, and we were plagued by mosquitoes and midges, so I did not sleep much. We could plainly hear the noise of continuous traffic on the Via Emilia, but whether it was going north or south we could not tell. The following morning was quiet, but we received a report that the Germans had arrived at the camp soon after we left. They arrested the Commandant and he was sent to a concentration camp in Germany. They ransacked our rooms, taking what they wanted mainly food and tobacco. They auctioned or gave away the rest to the villagers. At 1.00 p.m. the SBO told us that it was now too dangerous for everyone to remain together in the Bund, as we called the river and its banks. So Nos. 3 and 4 Companies and the Other Ranks Company would move that night and make for the hills. The remainder would probably go the next night. During the afternoon we heard the local people were offering civilian clothes to a proportion of the prisoners, who would then be taken to live on local farms. I was not keen on this. I was reluctant to change into civilian clothes because, rightly or wrongly, I thought there was a danger of being arrested as a spy and shot. Also I did not want to stay in that area.

During the day food had been coming in to us in surprising quantities. The local Italians brought bread and some Red Cross parcels salvaged from the camp. By the end of the day most people had about as much food as they could carry. This was the first time we had seen the marvellous goodwill and generosity of the Italian country people towards us as Englishmen.

The splitting up into small parties seemed to be going apace. So I thought about who I wanted as travelling companions. Scotty White and I naturally pooled up; Tommy Preacher had already been billeted out. I thought it would be useful to have a doctor with us in case of sickness. So I asked Jimmy James, who was a doctor in our company and who had made no arrangements to go with anyone else, to join us, and he agreed. Jimmy was a small dark Welshman with twinkling eyes. He had a great sense of humour, which was a bonus when we were in danger of taking ourselves too seriously. He normally let us take the decisions, but when we were undecided he would come with a quiet piece of advice which settled the issue.

The next morning, 11th September, we tried to plan our route for that night. I knew we had to cross the Via Emilia— the main road from Milan to Parma and on to Bologna and the railway which ran alongside it. Both were said to be patrolled. Later in the afternoon we met one of the prisoners who had tried to patrol up to the main road. He had been told by some Italians that there were sentries on all bridges, with motor cycle and aeroplane patrols up and down the road. They warned against trying to cross.

Major Fane Harvey, the company commander of the Other Ranks Company had listened to the English news. 8th Army was fighting its way north from Taranto, the Italians had taken up arms against the Germans, but there was no word of landings at Naples. Livorno, Spezia or Genoa. Altogether the news was not good.

Meanwhile Jack Moore had asked to join our party. He had been with some Sherwood Rangers officers, but they seemed very undecided as to what to do. He was keen on going to the hills. Jack was a cheerful, strong well built man. The fact that he had won an MM and received an Immediate Commission in the Field pointed to his qualities. I judged he would be reliable in difficult situations, and so it proved. He had plenty of ideas and displayed his initiative so often on our journey. He had an added advantage in that he spoke a little Italian. So we agreed to him joining us. Both he and Jimmy contributed in their own way to the success of our walk.

We had long discussions about which way we should go. The Swiss frontier was the nearest, but if we did succeed in crossing the frontier which was heavily patrolled, we would be interned. On the other hand it was a very long way to get through to 8th Army in southern Italy. A compromise was to go up to the hills and wait for the Allies to move north up to us. That meant crossing the Via Emilia which all reports said would be difficult. So we decided to go east for about twenty miles and south east down the east side of the country.

We had a meal and then set off north east down the Bund at 7.00 p.m. We were trying to get well clear of Fontanellato. After about three hours we stopped for a quarter of an hour and ate some grapes. We could only guess at the time as none of us had a reliable watch. Gradually we came into more open country with no vines, but large fields intersected by drains and canals. This made keeping direction difficult. Just after we had crossed a drain, we were passing a house when six men in shirt sleeves came out and asked us who we were. When we told them they asked us to come in. The place turned out to be the miller's house at Cna Barcaccia near San Secondo. The miller and his wife were very friendly, and with them was a

ASSISTED PASSAGE

Bersaglieri Lieutenant in civilian clothes who spoke French. We got on quite well with him and he did the interpreting with the miller, as our Italian was very poor. They offered us bread, cheese and wine which was very acceptable. We told them our plans, but they said it would be very difficult. We asked if we could stay there the night and the miller agreed.

We stayed where we were for the next two days, lying hidden in the fields during the day and sleeping in the mill at night. Meanwhile the miller's wife fed us very well. This hospitality and succour was to be repeated many times before the end of our journey. Many people came to talk to us during these two days; both civilians and soldiers who were trying to get away to avoid being called up by the Germans. The rumours continued. Some said the Swiss frontier had been opened to allow free passage to Allied prisoners. But all seemed to agree that the Germans were tightening their grip on northern Italy, requisitioning transport and ordering a night curfew.

We had a welcome surprise when the lieutenant brought two maps, one of the area we were in and the other slightly farther south. He also gave us a small compass, which was to prove useful from time to time on our walk south. We were now well set up. Our route south was still the subject of much discussion. Our intended route east and south east seemed to be more difficult than we had anticipated because of the large number of drainage channels, waterways and rivers we would have to cross. Also the main rivers, of which there were many, would be much wider than nearer their source in the mountains. So we decided to revert to our original plan of crossing the Via Emilia, in spite of the dangers of that, and making our way up to the hills west and south west of our present position.

Our supper was a meal of meat roll, bread and jam from our haversacks. Then we set off about 8.00 p.m. on 13th September for our first night march.

We Look to the Hills

THE moon was full when we started, and it was a lovely night for walking. Jack and I were in front with Scotty and Jimmy about 150 yards behind. I was very pleased to be on the move again with somewhere definite to make for. Personally I would have preferred to keep on walking until we rejoined our own forces, as I soon got impatient when we had to lie low for two or three days.

We were following a big land drain, which ran practically due south passing Fontancllato on the west, until we came to within about half a mile of the railway. Then we would swing out to avoid Sanguinara. For the first two hours everything went well, going a good three miles an hour with no scares. At one point we went off our route where the drain divided which was not marked on the map, which was made in 1909. However we came back to it after a mile or two. We reached the railway about 11.30 p.m. where we had a short rest. We were not quite certain where we were. Trains were passing about every quarter of an hour, and we could hear a motor cycle on the road coming at speed and then braking hard; two shots were fired, dogs barked and then the bike went on. We did not like the sound of that very much. We pushed on after about ten minutes, making a lot of noise or so it seemed to us. One drain we were following joined another and gave us good cover. We got right up to the edge of the line under the noise of a passing train. As we were waiting on the embankment we could hear Germans talking, but could see no sentries on the line; so over we went making quite a noise unavoidably. We followed the drain up through a farm for half a mile till we came to the main road. As there was no traffic at that moment we crossed without trouble, but we realised we were right in

Sanguinara which we had hoped to avoid. There was nothing to do but go on. A dog started to bark in a house we passed and I thought we would be spotted. A worry was that there was supposed to be a curfew after 8.00 p.m. We went up a ditch alongside a secondary road, through a garden and out into open fields again. I was glad when we were clear of the village.

We went on over the fields gradually gaining height. I thought of the verses from Psalm 121: 'I will lift mine eyes to the hills, from whence cometh my help. My help cometh even from the Lord, who hath made heaven and earth.' We came to a well with lovely clear water in a tub outside. We drank and put our heads in this—most refreshing.

We walked till about 4.30 a.m. having done about fourteen miles. As we were near the village of Costa Mezzana, we decided to wait there under the cover of a wood for the sun to come up, but became very cold doing so. Later a lady called Signora Adelaide hailed us as *'Inglesi—Liberatori!'* She and several others, men, women and children who came to see us, pressed us to stay and offered us civilian clothes. This we decided to accept, but I agreed only on the understanding it would be a temporary measure. A queer sight we looked. Jack was in a pair of blue overalls, Jimmy in a smart suit, Scotty in a white shirt and grey trousers, while I had an old pair of trousers and a coloured slipover shirt. We were divided between three households where we were given an evening meal. Later everyone collected in the main room of Signora Adelaide's house, where Jack and Jimmy did their best to answer the many questions put to us. At this time neither Scotty nor I could speak or understand Italian. However it was a pleasant evening. We slept in a loft in one of the farm buildings.

For a few days we went about in pairs, because we had heard that the Germans had prohibited any meeting of more than three people, although we had no means of checking if this was correct. In the evening we had another discussion about our plans, as we realised some of the locals were getting nervous about our presence in the area. They were worried about Fascists who they suspected would tell the Germans about what was going on. One suspected Fascist was an ex-major who was not popular in the district. However whatever the truth of the suspicions, he came to the house we were in to give us a good map of the whole of Parma province. He advised us to go to Bardi where there were several English speaking people.

The next day Signora Adelaide took us to see the men ploughing with oxen. The field was steep and difficult and the two white oxen were struggling. It was a slow business involving much pulling and shouting. It gave us a glance back into history. How strange to think that at one time all the ploughing was done in this way. Afterwards we helped a farmer gather walnuts. We were also treated to the sight of a girl treading grapes in a barrel with her not too clean feet. The barrel was about half filled with grapes, and then she picked up her skirts and vigorously marked time in the barrel. She seemed to know exactly when she had treaded enough and all the juice had been pressed out.

There was quite a merry party, with plenty of wine, attended by about fifteen people, and of course we were the centre of the stage. As we had decided it was time for us to move on, we changed back into our battle dress. We gave some of the locals chocolate and soap from our haversacks and in return received boiled eggs and bread.

We made an early start soon after 4.00 a.m. on 17th September and set off for Montemezio. Here we met Peter Barshall, John Hemmings and two other officers, all of whom had been at Fontanellato. We enjoyed the English news which we heard at a doctor's house, because we could understand it, and also we knew it was the genuine news, in contrast to most of what we had been hearing which was wishful rumour. There was still no signs of the Allies making landings in the north of Italy.

That night we did a night march of eleven miles past Varano di Marchese, over the river Ceno to Monte Camiano which is just south of Pellegrino, the place we were aiming for. It was sometimes difficult to find the way at night, and once we had to go back on our tracks, when we became involved in a steep wooded gorge. The next night we decided to walk on the roads, though Scotty and Jimmy were not happy with this as they thought it too dangerous. This enabled us to make good time to Facini and Rossi where we asked if we could sleep in a barn. The farmer refused saying there were too many Germans about.

Later that day, having decided it was safe to walk in daylight, we went along tracks to Chiappa and Praderi, through fine chestnut woods, eventually coming to a village near Capelli.

Here we met one of the most interesting characters we encountered in Italy. Signor Childa was a big, bluff and hearty man, who had shut up his tea shop near Victoria Station, London, at the outbreak of war. One could well imagine he was popular in the area and would make a success of his business. His son had been born in England. He showed us where two Englishmen were living. They were Flight Lt. Eric Ball DFC and Private John Schofield. They occupied a hut in a chestnut wood across a steep gorge from the village. They had been living in Capelli, but when the Germans came to Bardi, where incidentally we were recommended to go by the supposed Fascist ex-major, they thought this was too dangerous. They had been in Camp PG 29 near Piacenza.

We stayed with them for three days, food being brought up from the village. While we were there a cobbler from Bre, a village at least one and a half hours walk away, thinking we might need some boot repairs, brought his tools and a meal. As we ate it, he mended and studded our boots, which was most useful as mine were already showing signs of wear and were to cause trouble later on. It became apparent that everyone knew of our presence in the area, which made us feel rather insecure both for own safety and for those villagers who were helping us. Also we were making things more difficult for Eric Ball and John Schofield, particularly as regards food. So we said goodbye to them.

I was and always had been keen on pushing on south, but the others were against it. So we agreed to stay in the vicinity moving round from place to place, waiting for our troops to come.

On 24th September we moved east, climbing up and along the shoulders of Monte Borrigazzo (4,200 feet). This was the best walk we had had so far, looking down on the world around. To the north and north east was the lovely Ceno valley and the towns of Varzi and Bardi. In the other direction to the south and south east lay the river Taro with some high mountains beyond. From the map, and confirmed by direct view from this height, we decided that the valley of the river Pessola to the east was a good area in which to lie up. There were no roads up it, but we could see several good looking farm houses. However one could not reach it direct, and we had to go down the steep mountain side through beech woods first with chestnut at the lower levels. I had noticed that this arrangement of woodland species was common in this area. Chestnut woods seem to be found lower down, while beech is able to tolerate conditions at the higher altitudes. Right on the top is short turf, excellent for walking. We went down to the village of Costa which was a small group of houses inhabited by poor looking people. After trying at eight houses we managed to get into a barn for the night.

Between showers the next day we made our way towards Monte Dosso and reached Carnevalle which was two farms. At one was a fat old man who eventually agreed to us staying. He took a very pessimistic view of the war, and thought the British army would not be here by Christmas. Of course he was to be proved right; in fact they were not there by Christmas 1944. If we had taken more notice of him, perhaps we would have started walking south before we did. There seemed to be three families living in the same building and they numbered about fourteen. A pretty dark girl called Maria asked us if we were hungry and went off to prepare food. We ate this meal in a queer little room up some steps. This belonged to the second family. The meal was a *minestra* of bread and potatoes with grated cheese. It was now raining in torrents. Presently when everyone had eaten, they gathered in this small room. We got on quite well with our limited Italian, and photographs, names and ages were exchanged. Jack volunteered a song, the young Italians danced. Finally three of the girls sang songs at the top of their voices. In the confined space of this small room the level of sound was positively uncomfortable. However we slept well in some good straw at the top of a barn.

At Carnevalle we met the Molier family. He was an extrovert character and had worked at the Waldorf Astoria hotel, New York. His wife was ill with stomach trouble and Jimmy was asked to examine her. Signor Molier said we could stay a few days in his barn which was about half a mile away from the house; an ideal arrangement. The family put on an excellent lunch which was eaten with Waldorf Astoria cutlery! Later we helped the family to strip the leaves from maize cobs. All the girls from Carnevalle were there and it was quite a social occasion. The leaves are used for cattle bedding. Signor Molier seemed to be the *Padroni* or leading farmer of the place, and many of the local people work for him.

On another day we watched wool being spun. The wool is taken just as it is cut off the sheep without being carded. It is put on a bracket on a long stick. The woman gradually and quite slowly draws it out by spinning on a spindle till it is a fine cord. It is then wound on a stick.

After five days we decided we had probably been in the Carnevalle area long enough, and we did not want to outstay our welcome. So on 1st October we moved south east to a small hamlet called Bruschi. On the way Jimmy had been asked to see a relation of Signor Molier who had a septic foot. He boiled water and dressed it. Having a doctor with us, it is inevitable that he will get involved with the ills of the local people. At Bruschi we met two ex-Fontanella to officers—Lts. Robert Williams who had been in the next bed to me, and Terry Phillips. They were both in civilian clothes, as were several other ex-prisoners of war. They brought us up to date with the news, as they heard the English bulletins fairly frequently. There was a scare that day. A man on a horse, who was thought to be a Fascist doctor, was seen approaching the village. Everyone scattered, so we went off to the woods.

The 3rd October was a lovely hot, sunny day. So we went down to the river to wash ourselves and our clothes. After a good bathe we washed our shirts, underclothes and socks, and let the sun dry them and ourselves. It was the most pleasant day we had had since leaving camp.

We discovered we had left our water bottle at Bruschi, so went back for it. At the village we were told there was an English soldier who was very ill in the village of Costa D'Asino. We set off there straight away, and a woman showed us the track to take. It led up a ridge dividing the Pessola and Mozzola valleys. We walked through Bottione to Costa D'Arsino which we reached as it was getting dark. Here we met Flying Officers Black, Turner and Dawson and two batmen, all from our camp. They were very well settled and were being well treated in that village. We were surprised when they told us some families were quite comfortably off, as it looked to be a small poor place. One cannot always go by appearances. While Jimmy went to examine the sick soldier, the villagers said they would fix us up for the night. Jimmy came back with the bad news that he thought the soldier had a perforated appendix and therefore must have an operation within twenty four hours. His name was Private Burdett, he was 51 and incidentally had thirteen children! So the matter was serious. After having some food Jimmy went with two locals to Pieve, a village about two and a half miles away, to find an Italian doctor. Meanwhile Jack and I were struck by the air of independence and assurance of the family, to which we had been taken. The Germans were never mentioned.

The next day Jimmy returned with the news that there was no doctor at Pieve. Consequently there was no alternative to taking Pte. Burdett on a sledge to Valmozzola station, where he could be got onto a train to Parma. Pte. Burdett begged Jimmy not to leave him. The difficulty was that the station was manned by three Germans, and it was highly likely that Jimmy would have to give himself up to them in order to ensure Burdett's quick transfer to a hospital in Parma. We told Jimmy we would wait for him for a week in case he managed to get away. It struck me that Providence had guided us when we left our water bottle at Bruschi, had to go back for it, heard about one of our soldiers being ill, discovering he needed an operation and taking him off. Otherwise he would have died as no one at Costa D'Asino thought he was very ill.

In case there were any repercussions as a result of Jimmy and Burdett giving themselves up, we moved away from the village the next day. We intended to go to Pieve, but lost our way on bad tracks and in the bed of the river Pessola. So we crossed over and climbed up to Pessola village. I thought it was too soon to be back in that area near Carnevalle and the Molier's house. However we told them we had arranged to meet Jimmy there, should he be able to come back.

Scotty was now having trouble with his foot, which we discovered was septic. So we had to dress it three times a day. While there we watched the clipping of the sheep. It was done by the girls with ordinary scissors. They made it look easy, but took about a quarter of an hour to do one sheep, which no doubt would cause derision among English or Australian shepherds. But there was no need for expert quickness as there were only a few to shear. Afterwards we helped in the stripping of oak branches of their leaves which are used for bedding and fodder for cattle.

Every farm had prolific pear trees yielding delicious fruit, so we ate a lot of them. We were also given stewed pears quite often. Other meals were *minestra*—a soup which could vary from house to house. Sometimes it was thin, but more often a good broth with vegetables and pieces of meat. In fact sometimes it was more a stew than soup. *Polenta* was porage made of maize flour, stirred over a fire until it reached the right consistency, and then served with grated cheese and perhaps tomato sauce. Another common dish was *broder*—bread soaked in gravy or milk.

The week which we had promised Jimmy James we would wait for him had now passed. It was virtually certain he was back 'in the bag' as we used to say. So we decided we had hung about in this area for long enough, and Jack and Scotty had slowly come to realise there was nothing to be gained by staying. The Allied advance, delayed by clever German defence, was going so slowly that it is certain we would not see our troops in this area for some months. If we had known then what we learned later, that successful amphibious landings depend on being in range of one's own fighter cover and having sufficient landing craft, both of which precluded landings in north Italy at that time, we would have started walking south before we did. Also Scotty's foot was better.

So we resolved we would start walking south, possibly to the province of Umbria. I was very glad we had come to that decision as I had always wanted to move off to the south. I could or perhaps should have gone off on my own. But I could not bring myself to do that. Lack of courage or resource perhaps?

That evening we went up to Molier's house to say goodbye. His wife had been sent home from hospital, the doctors saying they could not find anything wrong with her. We were sorry to say goodbye to that family because they had been extremely kind to us. They were the best people we had met since leaving Costa Mezzana on 16th September.

ASSISTED PASSAGE

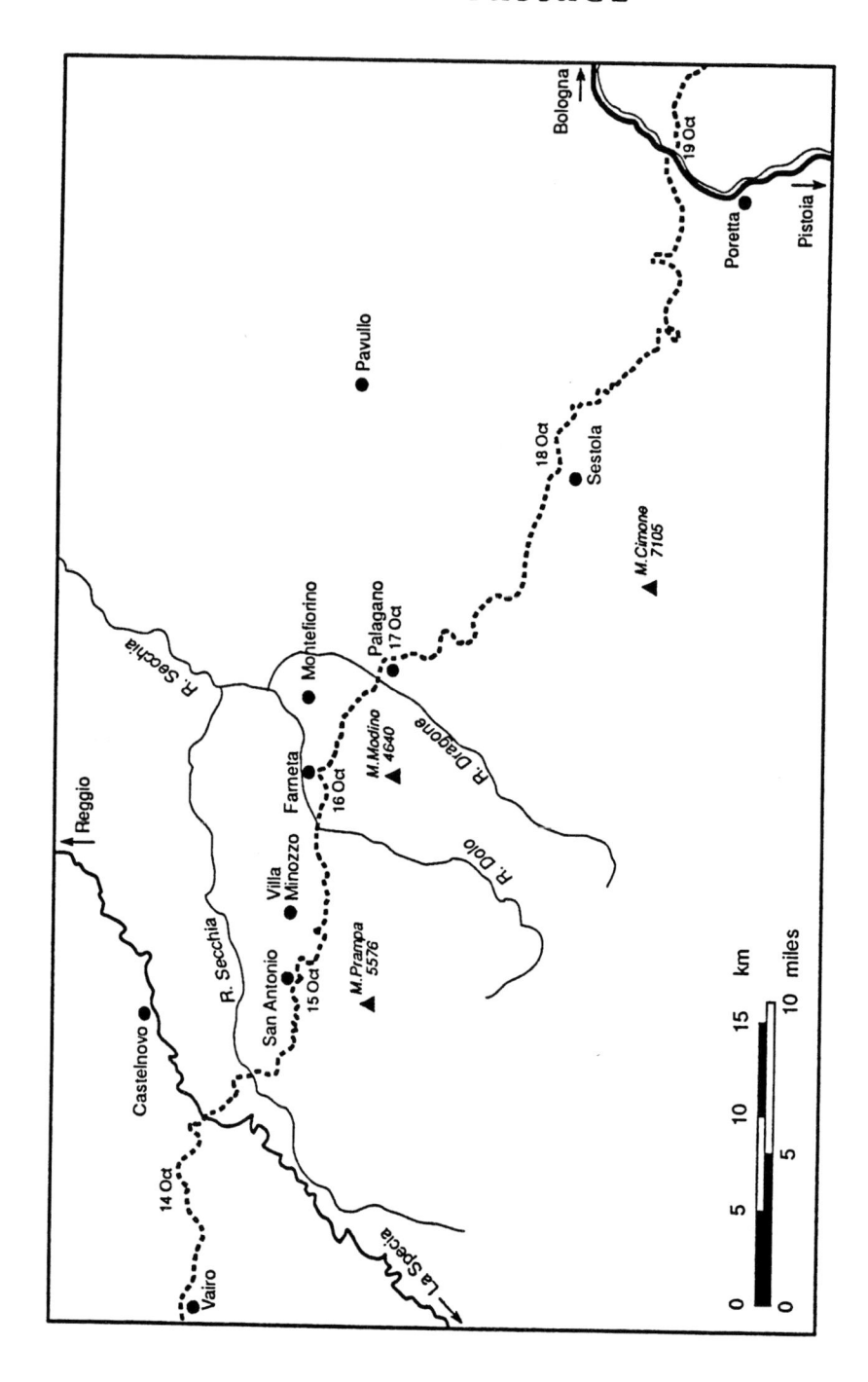

The March : Pessola to Perreto

WE were up early on 10th October and I was keyed up by the thought that we were at last starting our long walk. We collected as many pears as we could carry. The local people, several of whom we had got to know, did not really think we were going, or at least that we would be back before long.

Our first destination was the village of Pieve where we heard the people were friendly. We reached it about midday when the villagers were coming out of church, it being a Sunday. Near the church was the inn or *osteria* and from this out came an American who said he was a relation of Signor Moliere. He had been visiting Italy for his health and had been prevented returning to the States by the outbreak of war. He invited us into the inn. Already there was a noisy party in progress, with a number of men of all ages most of them the worse for drink. Several offered us wine.

Presently in came a well dressed man with a small beard. He was a lawyer whom we had been warned against because he was thought to be a Fascist. Of course, in Mussolini's time, to be a lawyer you had to call yourself a Fascist. He had been over to Pessola a few days before. However he seemed quite glad to see us. Soon an argument started with the lawyer completely dominating the stage. He made long speeches at the top of his voice with much waving of his arms. He always finished by saying '*Basta*'—enough, as if there was nothing more to be said on the subject. He would not listen to anyone else. The argument was political; he said how marvellously Italy was conducting herself and fighting with Britain and Russia against Germany. He had no great opinion of America, which

ASSISTED PASSAGE

annoyed the lame American who happened to be his cousin. This went on for about half an hour and was quite a pantomime. He called Scotty outside and gave him a hundred lira, which was generous. He then confided in us saying he was the local rebel leader, inviting us to be his staff officers. When the big day arrived, he and his men would rise up and attack the Germans we should then report to his headquarters which would be at Mariano.

Our attitude at the time to the lawyer and others we met, who claimed to be resistance fighters, was scornful. Our experience of most Italian soldiers was that they had no stomach for a fight. In hindsight we did the resistance people an injustice. Many of the Italian Partisan groups fought bravely in the later stages of the war and were a thorn in the side of the Germans. But in any case, even if we had had faith in these resistance people, we did not want to join up with them, but much preferred to try to get back to the British army.

The American pressed us to stay and said he would find us somewhere to sleep. But having said that, he went back to his game of cards. So we wasted a lot of time in the afternoon, and on that first day did only five miles.

Next morning we were woken by the agitated voice of the American shouting up to us in the barn where we had spent the night. He had heard the Germans were coming up the valley and we must go at once.

On this day we came to the river Taro, the first of many rivers the crossing of which was a potential problem. It was natural that in the valleys of the main rivers, and often running alongside them, were main roads and railways in some cases. Some of the bridges were guarded, and German army traffic was using the main roads and railways. Therefore we had to be careful about crossing these obstacles. We used to ask the locals the best place to cross, and were there any Germans about? If we could not get reliable information from the Italians, we would move down to a concealed position overlooking the river or road, and observe the traffic for an hour or so.

About 6.00 p.m. we went down towards the river Taro where a woman said we could go across on a basket. We went about five hundred yards upstream looking for it, when we met a man, his wife and son of about twelve all carrying sacks of maize. Having all taken our boots and socks off we waded over the river. The sharp stones in the river hurt our feet. When we had crossed, the man said he would show us over the road and railway, and asked us where we were staying the night. We told him we did not know but would find somewhere. As we were walking along near the railway a train carrying German army lorries came along. The man told us he worked on the railway between here and Valmozzola station, and he had seen much German equipment being taken by train to La Spezia. He said he had met Jimmy James and Pte. Burdett. He was going to take Burdett to the Germans at the station so Jimmy could get away. But Burdett had begged Jimmy to stay with him; so he reluctantly agreed. His unselfish act meant he again fell into German hands.

Our first long walk took us along high paths through chestnut woods shrouded in mist. We met a few local people who often gave us bread, cheese and occasionally cakes made of chestnut flour. We would ask about the best route. For instance the railway man told us to go north and east of Berceto, a small town ahead of us. But later we were told there were Germans in Berceto and the La Cisa Pass, a few miles to the south west, and we should go between the two. This had the added advantage that we had to cross only one road, the main highway between Parma and La Spezia. This we managed without difficulty. Then on over a high feature and through steep gorges to a lonely farm called La Casetta. We were not in walking trim yet, and were pretty tired at the end of the day. Sometimes the tracks and minor roads run in the right direction, which avoids cross country walking and makes a big difference to the distance covered in a day.

On the evening of 13th October we arrived at the village of Monchio della Corte, and a man who spoke good French, whose name we discovered was Bicci Giuseppi, asked us into his house before we had had a chance to enquire where we could sleep. One of the girls mended our socks. This kindness was an important benefit, as we knew we had to keep our feet in trim if we were going to accomplish this walk. Later, on two occasions we had temporary repairs done to our boots which were getting into a bad state, of which more later. Here we left our names and addresses, as the British Government had asked ex-prisoners of war to do, so that Italian people who had helped Allied nationals could be rewarded at the end of hostilities.

On 14th October we ran off the good map we had been given by the Italian Lieutenant near Fontanellato on 12th September, so we now had a problem keeping direction. We discovered that priests very often had a map. At Monchio della Corte the priest pointed out a good route on his map, through Vairo, Castelnuovo, Montefiorino, Montese to Firenzuola. As we neared each place we would ask the way to the next. By this means we managed to keep more or less to the general route we had planned. In fact I found it easier than expected to keep direction without a map.

We had a great variety of sleeping places. Usually we were put to bed in barns, and we became connoisseurs of good and not so good barns. Some were snug with deep, dry straw; while at the other end of the scale were draughty places with only a thin layer of straw, which meant we had some cold nights. We slept in a cowshed near the animals on 18th October. There was very little ventilation and it was stiflingly hot, partly from the heat of the cows themselves and partly because it was a warm night. Unless one has actually spent a night with cows, one does not realise the range of noises they make eating, chewing the cud and passing wind. Afterwards we named the experience of sleeping in a cowshed being 'being in the whale's belly.' In contrast on 14th October we slept in a bed; the first time we had done so since leaving the camp.

When we got up in the morning we always tried to have a wash, either in the house or at a tap in the yard. In order to preserve our very limited stock of razor blades, we shaved once every three days. But anything approximating to a bath was much more difficult. However on 15th October we came down to the river Secchia, a fast flowing tributary of the river Po running between steep banks. We realised we had to take our trousers off and wade over. So when we got to the other side we stripped off and had a good bathe. We did the same in a cold, clear mountain pool on 21st October. The cold took our breath away at first, but it was very refreshing and we liked to think we were a bit cleaner.

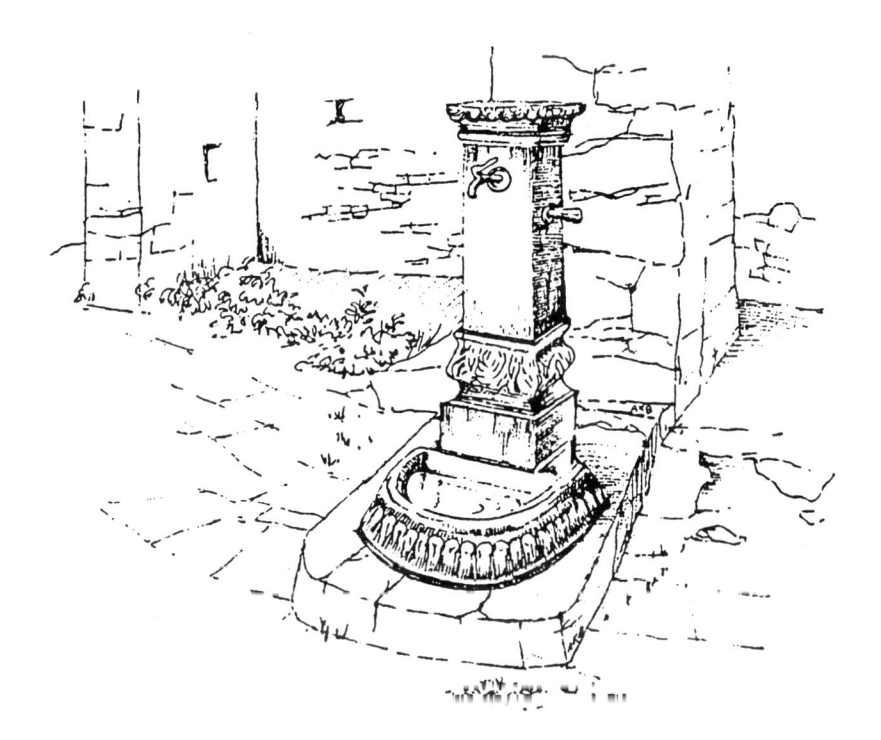

Typical village water pump where we often had a morning wash

ASSISTED PASSAGE

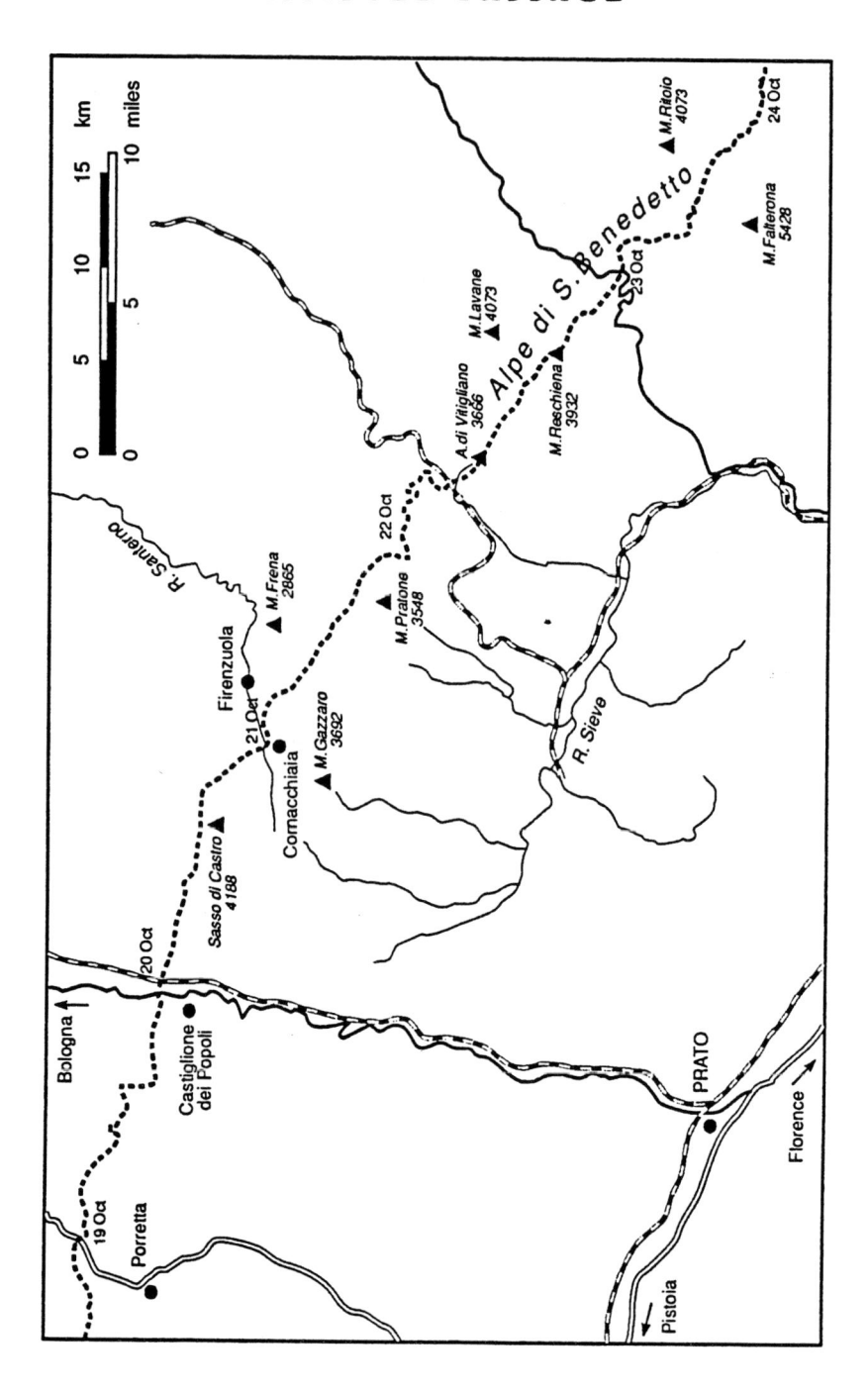

THE MARCH: PESSOLA TO PERRETO

As our route lay across the grain of the country we found ourselves going up to the next ridge, down to the next valley; up and down, up and down. It was tiring, but one was always keen to see over the next ridge.

Of course we met a large number of people on this journey. Both their questions and the subjects on which we were able to make ourselves understood, were always the same. Where were we going and where had we come from? In the evenings we tried to explain where our homes were in England, how we had been captured and what we did in the prison camp. Sometimes we found these encounters on the march delayed us, particularly if they were in the first half of the day. We had to stand and talk when we would be better putting more miles behind us. Often I was 'champing at the bit' to get moving and these delays irritated me.

Our reception and the kindness we received in San Antonio on 15th October was fairly typical of many villages in which we stayed the night. Most of the *contadini* seemed to have a natural or traditional wish to help travellers. Whether or not the fact that we were prisoners of war affected the situation is difficult to say. Perhaps it did—and to our benefit. At San Antonio the woman who had been walking with us asked us into her house and immediately started to prepare a meal. A lot of people came in to talk to her and us. She gave us an excellent meal of *pasta ascuita*, bread, cheese, grapes and wine. It was one of the best meals of our journey so far. Afterwards we sat and talked.

The next morning Scotty woke up with a heavy head cold and did not feel well. This highlighted an anxiety which we all felt, but which we generally kept to ourselves. This was that one of us would fall ill or have an accident, and what would we do then? That day we got wet walking through a persistent drizzle, and by the afternoon Scotty was feeling shivery and pretty miserable. However we managed to get in at the inn in the village of Farneto. The woman of the house took pity on us calling us *pauveri genti*. She lit a fire which dried our clothes to some extent. A soaking on a day's march became quite common especially later on, but we often managed to get near a fire to dry our clothes in the evening. At Farneto a very smartly dressed lady came into the inn and greeted us with 'good evening.' Scotty remarked that she spoke English well. She replied 'Yes, I am an American.' She was an opera singer. Because of the war, she and her Italian husband who was also an opera singer, had had to move first to Brazil and then to Italy. She kindly paid for our lodgings at the inn.

The first week's walking had shown us that we could generally agree about things. There was often some discussion about which road or track we should take. Occasionally there were arguments, but nothing too serious. In these cases, if the wrong track had been taken, it was better if the one who had not wanted to take that track did not say 'I told you so.'

The crossing of one of the most important arteries in this part of Italy—the main Bologna-Pistoia-Florence road—caused us a problem on 19th October. When we approached the road it was obvious there was a considerable amount of German transport using it. This was the first time we had seen German transport. We sat about twenty yards off the road and watched them going past. A vehicle passed about once every two or three minutes, and they seemed to be mostly German Air Force trucks. At first we thought we would have to wait till dark to cross, as the footbridge over the river was in full view of the road. However after waiting for about an hour, we reconnoitred to the left, went down a small stream, through a culvert under the road and along some low ground to the footbridge. We decided to risk crossing the river in daylight, and slipped across and under the railway on the far side without being seen by anyone in a German truck.

On 20th October at a nice house where we had been invited to have some food, we heard of two more officers from our camp. Lt. Colonel Burne and Lt. Churchill of 12 Lancers had been there a few days before. Later after a long climb up to a wild, flattish plateau we had a marvellous view of the

THE MARCH: PESSOLA TO PERRETO

surrounding country. On our right to the south east was Castiglione dei Popoli, a fair sized town where there were reports of Germans and Fascists. Running up the valley either side of it was the Bologna-Florence road. To the north the country gradually fell away to the Plain of Lombardy on which Bologna and Modena stand. Behind us to the west the country was high and wild rising to over 6,500 feet. After going downhill and fording the little river Brasimone, we crossed the main road without any difficulty, just by a milestone which said it was 40 kilometres to both Florence and Bologna.

That afternoon we met three men who said the British were eight miles from Rome and the Germans were asking for an armistice. One man said he had heard it on the radio himself. Rumours, rumours! We pondered on whether some Italians told us these stories because they thought that was what we wanted to hear, or whether there was a collective wish to believe the most wildly optimistic reports.

The next day we passed from Reggio Emelia province to Tuscany, marked by a stone on the roadside. The track went on up and took us into the mist and thick beech woods. The little compass came in useful here to ensure we were going in the right direction. Presently we came to a lovely clear pool, and although we were in the mist, decided to have a bathe and a good wash. Though it was very cold, it removed some days' dirt and freshened us up. Our route took us over Monte Sasso di Castro (4,190 feet) and Monte Freddi (4,270 feet). It was pleasant to be going down out of the mist and towards the valley. Jack went off to ask some farmers, who were busy ploughing, about the best way. We could see Firenzuola and the river Santerno which looked very wide. Jack was told that we had to cross a main road on which there was a lot of German traffic. But the Santerno would not be as difficult to cross as we thought.

When we reached the bottom, scrambling along a small stream, we found we could go under the main road. Another three miles brought us to the river Santerno. We asked a man

ASSISTED PASSAGE

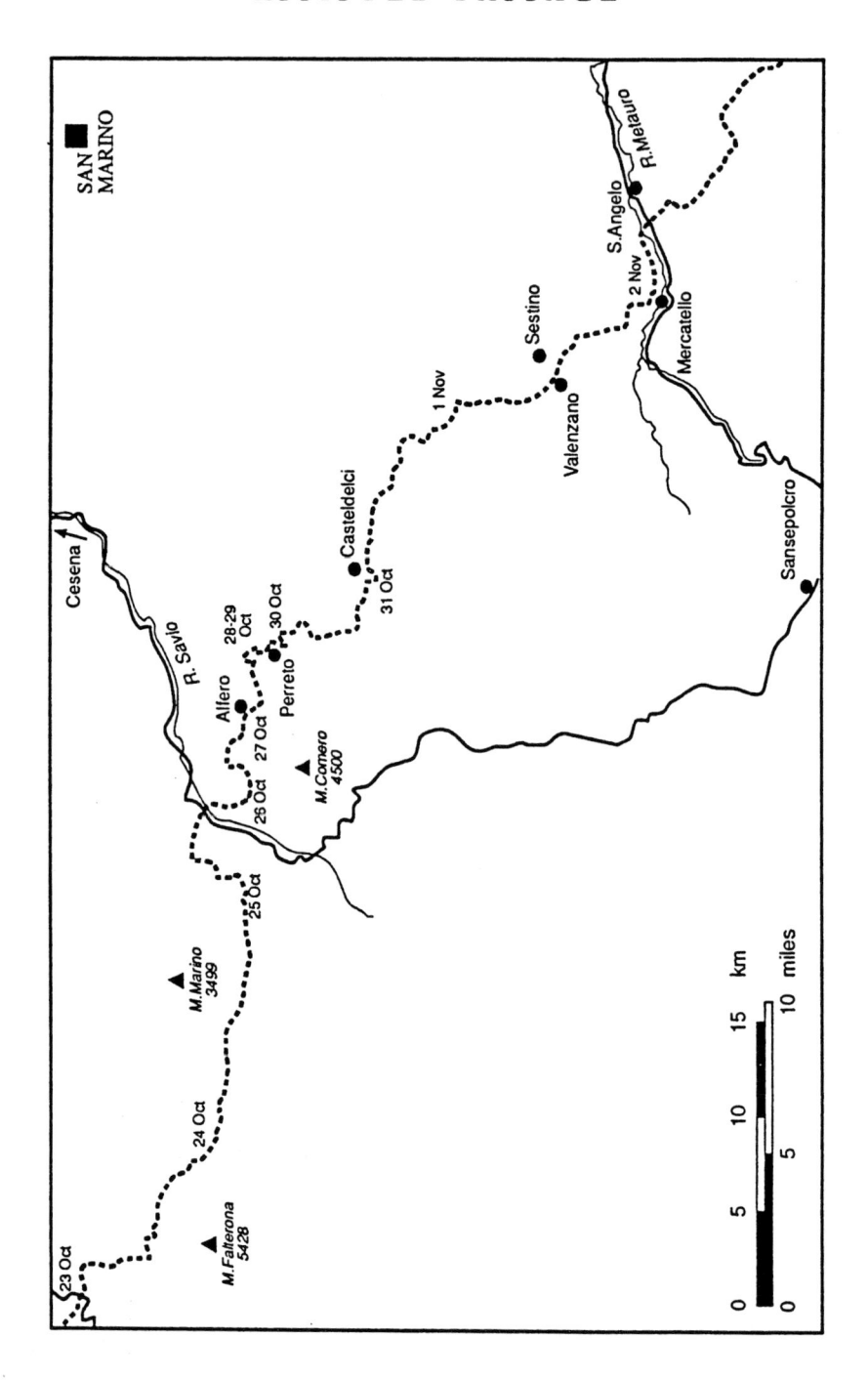

PLATE I

The Courtyard and front of the ORFANOTROFIO, *site of Campo PG49, Fontanellato*

QUESTA LAPIDE RICORDA
NEL QUARANTESIMO ANNIVERSARIO
I PRIGIONIERI DI GUERRA
INGLESI E ALLEATI
QUI INTERNATI NEL CAMPO
DI CONCENTRAMENTO P.G. 49
LA POPOLAZIONE DI
FONTANELLATO
CHE DOPO L'ARMISTIZIO
DEL 8 SETTEMBRE 1943
LI AIUTO' E LI NASCOSE
A RISCHIO DI
GRAVI RAPPRESAGLIE

FONTANELLATO 11 SETTEMBRE 1983

Plaque erected by the people of Fontanellato in 1983 in commemoration of the Allied prisoners of war and the many Italians who helped them

PLATE 2

The first house we came to in Poggio Cancelli (very much improved from its state on 14th November 1943)

The villages of Calaschio and (right on top of the hill) Rocca Calascio in which we stayed on the night of 20th November

PLATE 3

The village of Corvara. A typical Abruzzi village seeming to grow out of the barren hillside

The dam and waterworks where we crossed the Pescara river

PLATE 4

*The 'clay screes' which gave us so much trouble on our final walk.
Taken from the Guardiagrele—Pennepiedmonte road*

Casoli from above the east bank of the Lajo stream

the best way to cross. He said there was a footbridge. This we found, so crossed without difficulty and came to the pleasant village of Cornacchiaja.

Here everyone seemed interested in us. A man approached us who looked just like 'John Bull,' dressed in plus fours and with a small pointed beard. He took us to the priest's house where we heard the Italian News. The priest then produced a map which covers this area in great detail, and he showed us a good route. Thereupon he gave us the map, a most useful and generous present. He took us through to the kitchen and sat us down to a really good meal—*pasta ascuita*, cold pork, delicious pears and red wine. Afterwards we were led to a large house belonging to an Italian author named Tito Casino. As we wrote out our names and addresses for him, he told us that two other officers from Camp 49 had stayed with him. We wondered why they had moved on when he showed us the bedroom we were to sleep in. It had a double bed, brushes and boot polish and a proper flush lavatory, the first we had seen on our journey. What luxury! Though the temptation to stay was great, we thought we must move on the next day.

Our ability to cover good distances each day very much depended on the difficulty of the going. For instance on 22nd October we had some very steep climbs and a descent in to an awesome gorge, which we managed only by hanging onto the trees. This was extremely tiring. But thanks to the map we had been given at Cornacchiaja, we reached a secondary road and made good time on it for about two miles.

In contrast, on the next two days 23rd and 24th October, after a steep climb through beech woods we reached the ridge of the Alpe di San Benedetto, where we followed good tracks along the shoulders of one mountain to the shoulders of the next. Thus we went over seven mountains from Alpe di Vitigliano (3,200 feet) towards Monte Falterona (5,400 feet). On the way we saw a magnificent sight. Below us on our right was the valley of the river Sieve, a large tributary of the river Arno; and beyond, the valley of the Arno itself leading towards Florence. Both valleys were filled with white clouds, while all around the mountains stuck out of the white mass like islands in a sea of cotton wool. The ridge we were on forms the boundary between Reggio Emelia province and Tuscany. The country is mountainous and the sides are clothed by thick beech and chestnut woods. It is difficult country for walking, unless one can strike a good path such as the one we were on, taking one along the features rather than across them. Also the views from the tops were magnificent, and one was filled with a sense of exhilaration from walking 'on top of the world.'

In that part of the country, however, the farms were few and far between. We had spotted a lone farm from some distance away and it seemed the only place we could stay. When we asked the farmer he was unwilling. We were loath to go on to find somewhere else as we were very tired. It was the only time we had to exert some persuasion. We told him he was the first man we had met who was frightened of the Germans, and pretended to take his name. After that he pressed us to stay! His wife seemed more kindly disposed to us than her husband, and she busied herself preparing a meal. After supper the farmer started to make boots, so I asked him if he could repair mine which were in a pretty bad state. He made a good job of patching the right boot with another piece of leather. This was to prove useful in the weeks ahead.

We had another encounter with British servicemen. We walked some way with Lieutenants Maurice Goddard and Eric Hampson who had been in Fontanellato with us. Then there were three English soldiers in civilian clothes who had been captured in France in 1940, taken to Germany, escaped from there into France, arrested by a French pro-Vichy gendarme, taken to Nice where they were handed over to the Italians and finished up in the camp at Modena. After all those adventures they escaped from Modena at the Armistice, though most of that camp were taken to Germany. We also met three Australian soldiers, and a man named Jackson who came from Durham City and whose brother had been a driver in my Carrier platoon in 1940. This man had jumped off the train taking him to Germany. Another interesting meeting was with a Guardsman who had been captured in the Guards Brigade attack on the Horseshoe feature at Mareth. He had got away from a working camp near Florence and was now working on a farm in the vicinity. All these men had interesting stories to tell, and several had shown considerable initiative in getting away.

About this time Scotty developed a very painful knee. He stoically kept going but it slowed us up. Near the river Savio which we crossed on boulders, are large sweet chestnut woods. At a farm where we stayed the night of 26th October, there were eighteen people in the house of whom about twelve were girls from a nearby town, who had come to help gather the chestnut harvest.

The four days 27th to 30th October were very wet. It seemed that the weather had broken and the autumn was over. We reflected ruefully that this walking was all right in fine weather. In fact one could almost say that so far we had enjoyed a walking tour of the northern Apennines. But it was no joke in pouring rain when we had no waterproofs and no change of clothing. We got very wet, in fact wetter than at any time on the journey so far. Consequently we made slow progress on these four days because we tried to shelter where we could, and also because Scotty's knee was rather worse and he could only hobble along. He tried putting hot and cold dressings on it in the evenings which helped a little. What we needed was a good barn where we could lie up for a day or two to rest Scotty's knee. On these wet days it was difficult to know what to do. We were reluctant to go on in pouring rain, but equally we did not want to overstay our welcome. I became very frustrated by these delays. I seemed to have a physiological urge to push on, rather like some birds get the migratory urge in autumn and spring.

At Alfero we met a Dutchman and his son who were Jews and refugees from Florence. He was connected with shipping and spoke very good English besides French, German, Spanish and Italian. He had some 1/500,000 Italian Touring Club maps, from which I made out what seemed to be a good route, listing all the main places as far south as the river Pescara. The Dutchman made the interesting comment that the English propaganda broadcasts to Germany were the best of their kind on the air. The priest, at whose house the Dutch people were staying, said we could spend the night at his *padroni's* house. A *padroni* is the man who runs the priests' farm. Most of the priests in the larger villages have one. I am afraid his barn where we spent the night was draughty and had very little straw. So we were cold and uncomfortable.

On 30th October we walked a short distance to the village of Perreto. As we were absolutely soaked, we called at the priest's house and asked if we could come in to dry our clothes. The people were not very friendly, thinking perhaps we were Germans, though we made it quite clear we were English. In the house was a woman who was an evacuee from Pisa. She complained bitterly about the British and American bombing which never hit any military targets, and that we always machine gunned women and children in the streets! Later we spent a cold, damp night on poor straw in a small barn. This was one of our worst days. Nevertheless we had to remind ourselves that these people had no need to take us in, and were kind and brave to do so.

We had now been walking for three weeks. We thought at the time we had made fair progress, but realised the hardest part was still in front of us. Although we had no means of measuring it at the time, we had done a hundred and sixty two miles from Pessola, an average of about eight miles a day. This does not sound very much, but considering the many delays we encountered on route and the problems of finding the best way, it was not unreasonable.

The March : Perreto to Corvara

THE rain had finally stopped by Sunday 31st October, so we decided to continue our walk, our first destination being Casteldelci. Several times we were doubtful of the route to take at a cross tracks, but almost invariably someone came along who we could ask. At the priest's house in Casteldelci we met two British majors who had been in Camp 29, Majors Marshall, Seaforth Highlanders, and Syme, Royal Artillery. Syme was an Old Oundelian and both knew Ross Mclaren who had been in their camp. The next day they managed to get some repairs done to their boots. Meanwhile Scotty went to see the doctor as his knee was still painful. But he could not do anything for him and merely painted the knee with iodine. We reached the hamlet of Casa Barbona on the evening of 1st November—a year after Scotty and I had both been involved with the Operation Supercharge attack at Alamein.

The next morning one of the men offered to cut our hair. We must have looked awful, as our hair had not been cut since leaving camp and had become long and untidy. He was quite a skilled barber and we looked more presentable as a result. That day we had two good guides. The first was an old man who took us on small paths and sometimes across country to the village of Valenzano where some friends of his lived. We were not sure whether his bringing us to the village was because he wanted to see his friends, as much as to avoid the Germans. The second guide was a young man of about twenty who took us on good upland paths and minor roads towards San Angelo and Mercatello. Before he left us we came to a good view point from where he indicated our route ahead.

ASSISTED PASSAGE

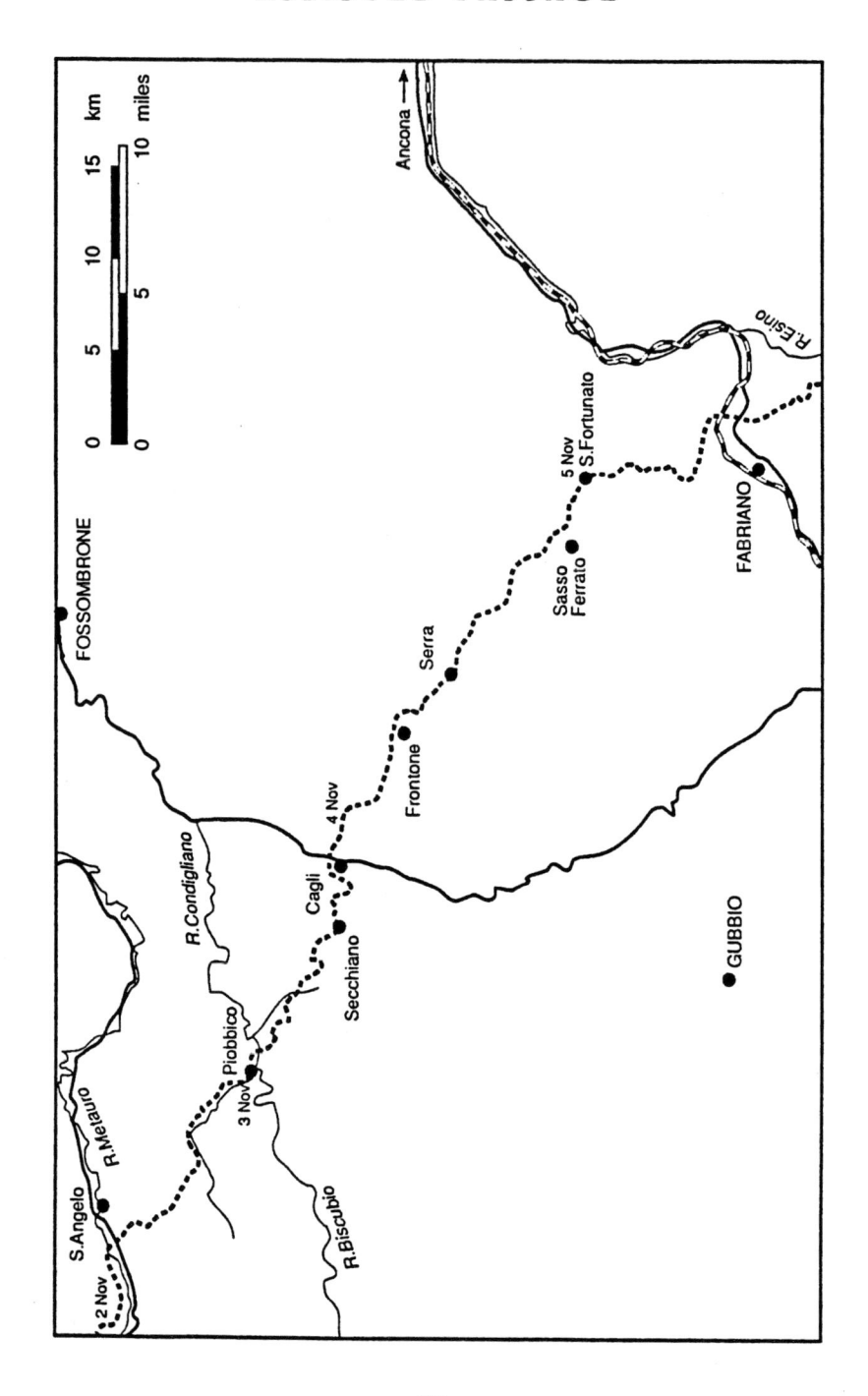

THE MARCH: PERRATO TO CORVARA

On occasions the Italians mistook us for Germans, and it was interesting to watch their reactions both initially and later when they learnt we were English. On 3rd November the Italians believed so strongly that we were German that two Yugoslav refugees took fright and ran off to the woods. One could perhaps understand it, as we were still in battle dress and Scotty was fair haired. The small town of San Angelo now appeared ahead of us. It lay in the wide valley of the river Metauro, the valley being lined with neat rows of vines. The church towers rose above the close cluster of grey houses. Behind all this were the hills looking green and not unwelcoming. It was a scene one sees on travel posters.

It was my turn to feel achy and shivery. So I could have done without the trouble we had in crossing two rivers. We could not find a bridge over the river Candiglione and had to wade, a cold unpleasant experience in the semi darkness. It was completely dark when we came to the wide river Biscubio. Again we were forced to take off our boots and socks and wade. Then to make matters worse we had great difficulty in finding somewhere to spend the night. After trying the priest and three other houses, we were fixed up in a cowshed belonging to another house. In the evening I asked for some hot water and added some sugar and brandy from my flask. This did me some good. We learnt the peoples' nervousness was the result of some British parachutists having dropped in the vicinity about a fortnight ago, and the Germans had come to the villages searching for them.

We had gradually come round to the view that we were more likely to be recaptured wearing khaki battle dress, and we might also be exposing the Italians who helped us to unnecessary danger. The subject came up in the village of Sechiano on 4th November and some of the women were very surprised we were still in British uniform. I hoped we could have our battle dress dyed because it was so much warmer than the civilian clothes we were offered. But that did not seem possible, so after much discussion we all agreed to

ASSISTED PASSAGE

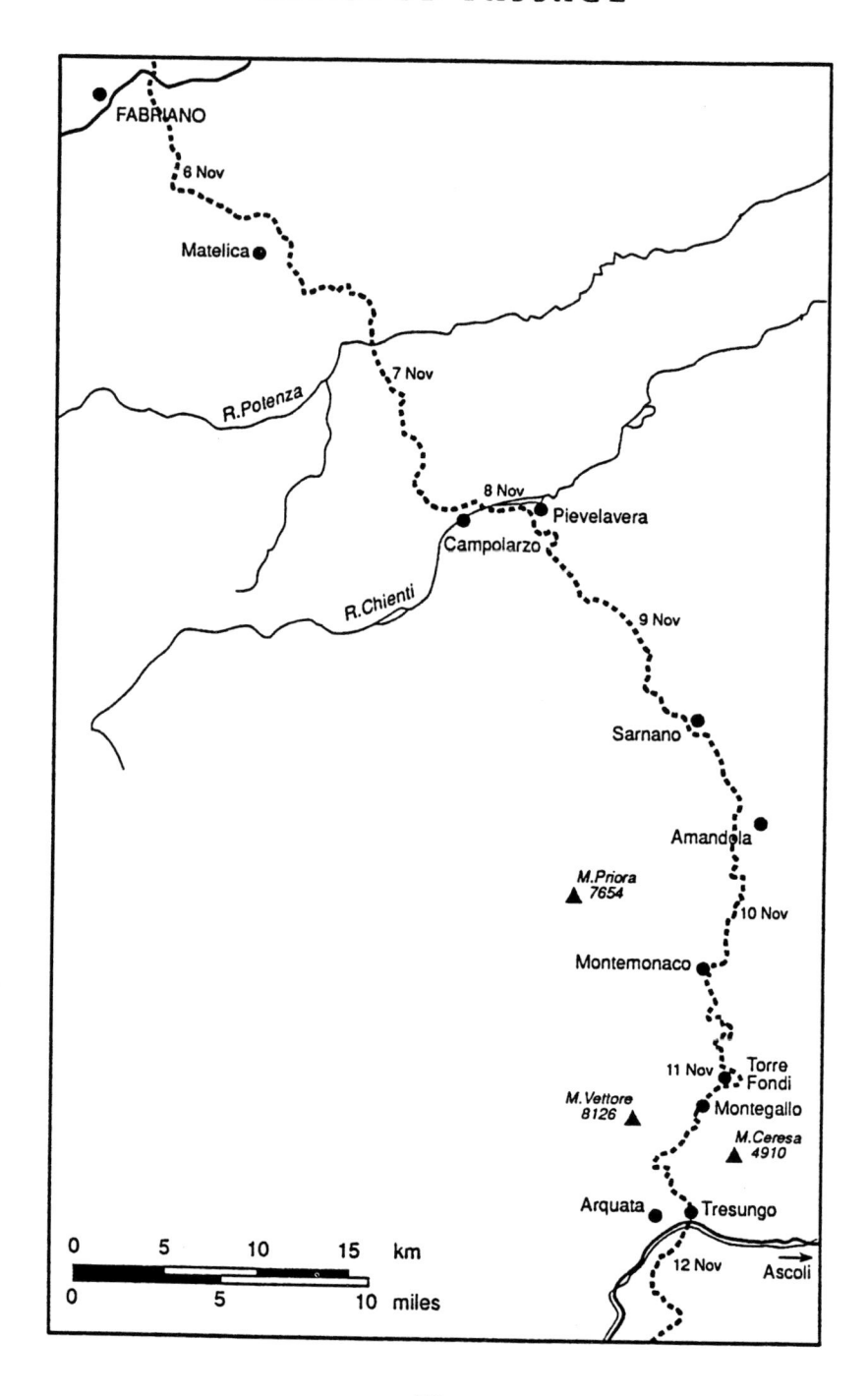

change into civilian clothes. Some of the villagers took us to different houses where we were offered various items of clothing in exchange for our battle dress blouse, trousers and shirt. I was given a vest, a shirt with no collar, a thin pair of trousers and a jacket. Scotty had much the same except his jacket was a blue check and was so thin you could see through it when it was held up to the light. Jack's kit was better except his trousers were patched. We certainly noticed the difference in warmth, but we gradually got accustomed to it.

Later that day we came to the river Burano and walked along the bank some way looking for a place to cross dryshod. Finding none we had no alternative but to wade. The water was above our knees, but we got across all right and then walked into the little town of Cagli, a charming old world place with several attractive churches standing up above the houses.

Now we were in civilian clothes we foolishly thought we looked like Italians! We had more confidence in walking along roads. Just as we were approaching Sassoferrato a horse drawn bus crowded with passengers with more hanging onto the sides, drew level with us. The driver leaned over and shouted 'Going to town, Johnie?' So much for our disguise! But the day finished well. Avoiding Sassoferrato as it was likely to contain Germans, we came to the village of San Fortunato. At the priest's house we were able to dry our clothes in front of his fire. He then took us to hear the News in English which was quite a thrill. The news seemed quite good; the British army was approaching the river Trigno north of Termoli, the next obstacle in their advance. The priest's housekeeper put on a most welcome meal of *minestra* with wine and apples to follow. It was the first hot meal we had had for five days. To crown a good day's walking we were offered a double bed for the night. Though a bit crowded with three in it, we all had a good sleep.

The valley of the river Eshio is a large wine producing area. The country is covered with rows of vines which we found it difficult to walk through. We could not take a straight line between two points, but had to zigzag along the lines of vines. The farms were only about three hundred and fifty yards apart. At nearly every farm the people were most insistent that we drank a glass of wine with them. They made about two thousand litres a year and so drank it almost continuously. At this time of early November the wine was new and not very nice. The next day I discovered that raw wine is a most potent laxative, and had a bad bout of diarrhœa. In the Esino valley when we were walking near a railway, a train came past and we heard shots being fired and some came quite near us. I thought it was someone shooting hares, but we looked up and saw ten or fifteen Germans standing on a flat rail truck just blazing into the countryside. I did not know what the idea was, frightening the people perhaps, or they were bored and arranged some mild excitement to pass the time.

On each day's march we crossed one river after another; first the Esino, then the Potenza and then the Chienti. As we moved south the presence of the German army became more obvious. Consequently some of the Italians were, quite naturally, more reluctant to invite us into their houses or allow us to sleep in their barns.

However fortune favoured us on 8th November. It came on to rain heavily as we joined a main road at the village of Campolarzo, so we sheltered in a sort of outhouse for an hour, and had a bite to eat from the food we were carrying. German trucks and cars were passing along the road periodically. When the rain slackened we decided to risk walking on the road. There was nowhere to get off it, though we knew that if an alert German in a truck passed us we might be picked up. Later the rain came on again and presently it was coming down in sheets. My stomach was still out of order and I was feeling far from well. We crossed the deep, fast flowing river Chienti and walked along a track to the village of Pievefavera, where we met a man watering a horse and he took us to his house. After sitting in front of his fire for about two hours we were nearly dry again. There was no sign of the weather clearing and no hope of us moving on that day. The house was nicely furnished and the owner seemed prosperous. This was confirmed in the evening when they gave us a very nice meal, well served with polished silver and glasses. This was an unusual treat for us, as indeed was the use of a proper lavatory in the house. The old man took us to his barn about four hundred yards from the house, and we had a good sleep in some new straw.

We were now walking through country in which one of the main crops is olives. All the cooking is done with olive oil, which at first was not to my taste, but I got used to it. We had our first experience of snow on 11th November. As we set off we had a superb view of the summit of Monte Priora (7,650 feet) about five miles away. The peak was covered in snow and made a very picturesque sight. But it was also rather disturbing, as it was a sign that winter was coming on and at the back of our minds lay the fear that we might be immobilised by snow. Later that day the tracks we were following over high ground were covered by about three inches of snow.

At the small village of Forgo we met three English soldiers, one of whom had a handkerchief map given to him by a British paratrooper. In this village was a cobbler's shop which seemed to be the central meeting place of the village. My boots were now in a bad state, with the sole of one coming away from the upper and a bad crack in the upper of the other. The cobbler took one look at them and said they were not worth repairing. So we each had to make do with buying a pair of laces from him. The one thing which was extremely scarce in Italy at this time was footwear and boots in particular. So there was no chance of my getting another pair.

At Forgo we met a big tall Yugoslav officer who had a 1/500,000 Italian Touring Club map, and from this I made out a route as far as the river Pescara. This man said he had been farther south to try to get through the lines, but it was hopeless. According to him every road and path was blocked by pro-German Fascist Militia, who were looking especially for prisoners of war. He strongly advised us against going on. I do not know if he was trying to frighten us, but that report was obviously exaggerated. Thousands of militia would be needed to block all roads and tracks. However Jack was impressed with the fellow and thought we had reached the point where we had better stop and wait for the British army to come up to us. I could not agree and said we should go and see for ourselves first before turning back. We had quite an argument about it. Scotty rather agreed with me, so we decided to go on. The Yugoslav told the Italians they should start a guerilla war against the Germans as the Yugoslavs had done. But the Italians would have none of it.

One of the English soldiers offered to take us to the next village, Torre Fonde, where another four soldiers were living. They were grand fellows and were very popular with the village folk who looked after them well. They immediately busied themselves arranging a meal for us, and said we could sleep in their empty house which had beds in it. We also met an Italian ex-pilot who was studying English and could speak it fairly well. He spoke English to us while we did our best to reply in Italian. Before we went to bed we were treated to the magnificent sight of Monte Vettore (8,130 feet) with its snow covered peak sparkling in the moonlight. The mountain seemed very close towering above us, but it was actually four and a half miles away. Again the following morning everyone was kindness itself and we found it difficult to get away. We agreed that if we cannot get through the lines, we would return to Torre Fonde to await the Allies advance.

As we were walking along the secondary road from Montegallo to Arquarta we saw four Spitfires circling overhead, and presently two of them shot up a German convoy on the main Ascoli-Spoleto road, setting fire to three trucks. This was a real boost to our morale and made us feel we were very near our own forces. However we envied the pilots who no doubt would soon be drinking tea in their comfortable mess.

The Italians were naturally very curious about us. Often we wanted to walk straight through a village, perhaps because we were behind time and did not want to be delayed, but this was usually impossible, people stopping us to ask the usual questions: who were we, where had we come from and where were we going?

As we approached yet another river—the Tronto, we wanted to ask about the best place to cross, and were told to make for the village of Tresungo. We made our way down by small paths and were about to cross the main road at Tresungo when a woman came up to us jabbering in Italian. She was absolutely hysterical, and it was very difficult to make out what she was saying. We eventually gathered that we must not cross the road as there were about twenty German trucks in the village. When our planes strafed the convoy the Germans pulled into the village and were waiting there. This was an example of us being immediately recognised as not being Italian. We were grateful for the woman's warning. We went back up the hill to a hut in which she said we should spend the night. I was in favour of going on as soon as possible, but eventually agreed it was wiser not to. We finally decided to go on at dusk.

Afterwards I went down nearer the road and to a flank where I could look into the village. Some German trucks were still parked there. I then saw a party including the woman carrying food up to the hut. So I followed them up. Amazingly they had brought a large meal of *minestra*, several loaves and a big bottle of wine. Scotty was not very hungry, but Jack and I had a good meal as did two Royal Artillery sergeants who had joined us. We put some of the loaves into our sack which was now rather heavy. An old man who had come up with the woman wanted us to stay the night in the hut. But we were keen to go on. So at 5.30 p.m. he went down to the village and we were to follow ten minutes later, when he would signal if the Germans were still there. This worked well, and he showed us a way across the river, leaping from one rock to

ASSISTED PASSAGE

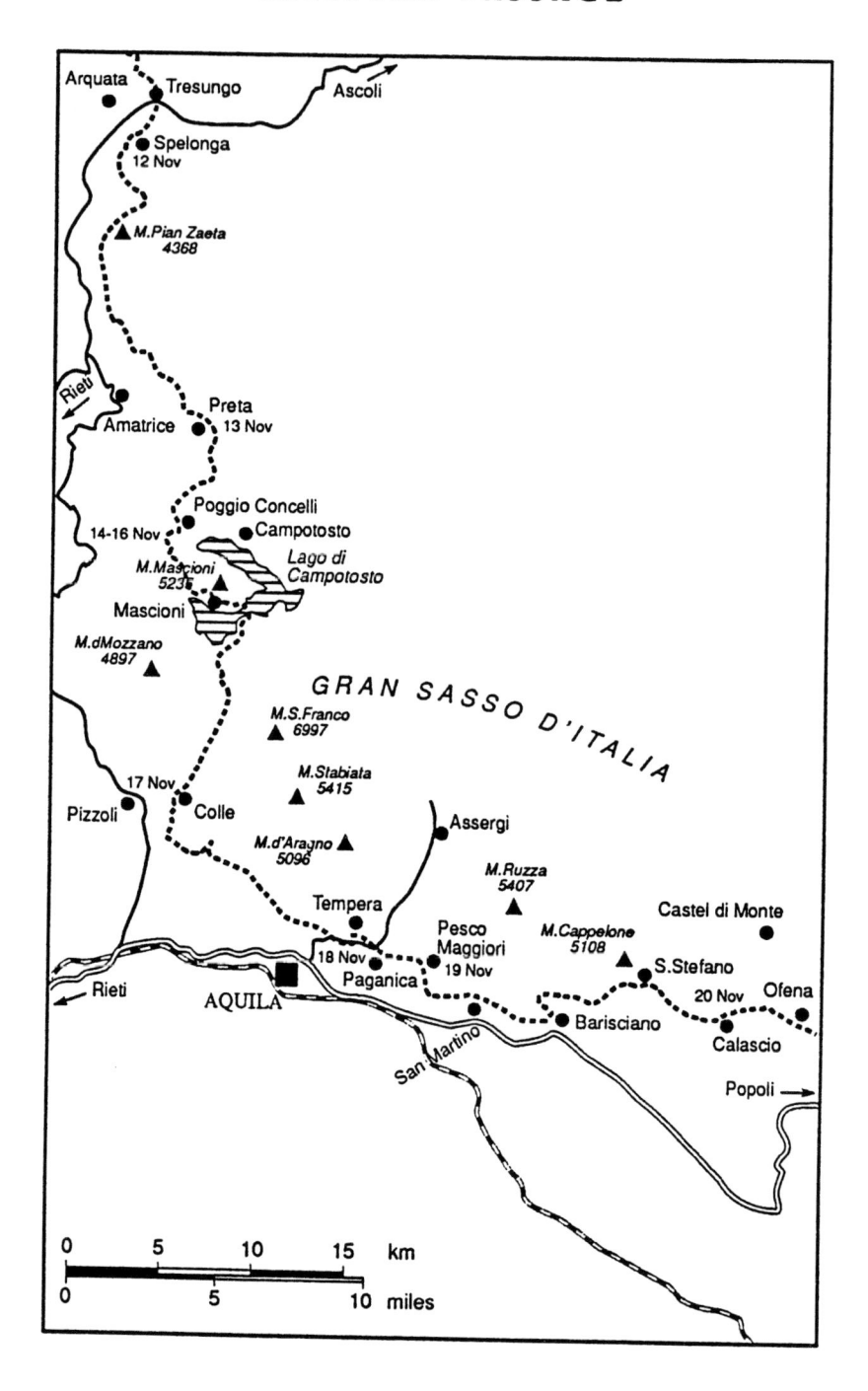

THE MARCH: PERRATO TO CORVARA

another. We were thankful that that was another major river behind us. Soon after, we came to Spelonca where we were invited to stay in the house of a man who had lived in America and spoke English fairly well. That night we had the luxury of the three of us sleeping in a double bed with the two sergeants on the floor.

On the next day 13th November we had a steep climb up to Monte Pian Zaetta (4,366 feet) and on our left above us was Monte L'Inversaturo 5,613 feet)—outliers of the Gran Sasso range. On the high ground we walked in six inches of snow. We were now in Abbruzzi. Many of the people in these parts live above 3,500 feet and make their living from horses and sheep. Almost no corn or wine is produced. We had a stiff walk against a gale force wind with heavy rain along an exposed plateau. As we were now soaked through we determined to try to find somewhere to dry off in the next village, which we thought was Campotosto. We went up to the first large house in the village, and were taken up three flights of stairs to a kitchen. Everything in the house was of stone, and about as comfortable as a mediæval castle. However the old woman made up the fire and soon our clothes were steaming. We discovered the village was Poggio Cancelli, not Campotosto.

We learnt there had been a Prisoner of War Working Camp nearby, and some of the escaped soldiers lived in the village. In the afternoon some of these came in. There were six Cockney lads living in an empty house, two nice Scotsmen lived somewhere else and there was a further six about the place. At one time there had been forty eight, but several had drifted away. Campo PG 145 had housed about a hundred and fifty men who were set to work on a big water undertaking. Conditions had been rather harsh. When the Armistice came there was no clear leader, and the men were undecided as to what to do. The Germans arrived after two or three days and many of the men were interned again.

ASSISTED PASSAGE

Others were in the village and managed to get away, but some were recaught when the Germans went up the mountain after them. The men said about a third of the camp was retaken. The Germans had done a bit of shooting which frightened everybody. Still living in the village was an Italian lieutenant who had been the camp adjutant, the camp doctor and a Carabiniere officer. Later that evening we met them and had quite a pleasant time with them. Our soldiers said the three Italians had treated them well and been helpful since the Armistice.

The next day it was snowing hard and there was no question of our moving on. The empty house where we had spent the night with the six Cockney soldiers was cold and rather uncomfortable. There was a fire, but all nine of us could not be in front of the fire at once, so it was a matter of taking turns. We gathered the food situation was rather precarious. In spite of this the soldiers were not keen to move on, preferring to wait until the British arrived. We heard that a bus had come to the village which would be going to Rome the next day. So Jack and I went to find the driver to see if he would take us part of the way. As we were looking for the driver we met the Italian lieutenant again—his name is Joseph Nicolai—and he told us there was no chance of us getting on the bus as it was always full. Later I was able to take my boots to the local cobbler. They were now in a dreadful state, both soles worn through and a large hole in the upper of the right one. This meant I had almost permanent wet feet. But the cobbler could only patch them up to a small extent.

The snow continued most of the night and lay deep the next morning. We had to curb our impatience about moving on. I had always worried that we would get snowed up and this village was not a good one for that. The food situation was too precarious, which was not surprising considering the number of extra people living in the village. It was a wonder that the locals managed to feed everybody as it was. Also I must confess we were getting rather tired of the very broad Cockney lads' conversation. During the morning we heard of a muleteer who guided people down past Aquila and through the line. When we found him, he said he knew all the tracks as far as the river Pescara. Unfortunately he was not going himself, but he gave us a good route. That evening Lt. Nicolai told Jack very confidentially that he would give us a blanket each when we set off. We slept beneath a light covering of straw, but the nights were very cold.

The street in Poggio Cancelli where Lt. Nicolai lived

ASSISTED PASSAGE

On the morning of 17th November the weather had cleared though snow still lay thick on the ground. We decided to move on. Before starting we collected the blankets from Lt. Nicolai. They were Italian army issue and were quite good. We were given two small and one large one. The only place we could carry them was in Scotty's sack which made it heavier than ever. This meant we had to take it in turns to carry it. Joseph Nicolai had a collection of the names and addresses of officers and soldiers who had been through the village and who he had helped. He was keeping it to show to the British authorities. I had his home address in Bari, Scotty took the Carabiniere's in Taranto and Jack had the doctor's in Lecce. We said when and if we got through we would try to let their people know where they were. In the event we found there was no civil postal service in operation, so were unable to do so. We also had the names and addresses of all the British soldiers in the village.*

We left Poggio Cancelli about 9.15 a.m. and our route lay over Monte Maschioni (5,170 feet) to Mascioni village. Soon we passed near Campo PG 145, looking very derelict in the snow. The ascent was pretty steep and the snow became deeper the higher we climbed. About halfway up it was at least three feet deep and we were struggling hard to make only very slow progress. Jack took the heavy sack from Scotty and Scotty and I took it in turns to go ahead to make the track. Nowhere would the snow bear our weight and towards the top it was above our waists. Quite suddenly we would sink into a deep drift and have a frantic struggle to get out again. After a very slow exhausting climb with many pauses for rest, we reached the top. As we started to go down the other side Mascioni, lying between the mountain and a large lake, came into view. Having reached the top our troubles were not over. Going downhill we were in danger of slipping a considerable

---

* On the 9th October 1944 I received a letter from Lt. Nicolai written from Bari. He had got home on 1st July 1944.

distance. After a very difficult descent we reached the track along the lakeside leading to the village. We saw a woman waving at us and she seemed to be shooing us away. Then we realised this was the Italian way of beckoning us. We were asked into her house, given a plate of *minestra* and were able to partially dry our clothes, which of course were soaked from walking through the snow.

The soup did us a power of good and we set off again about 2.00 p.m. After our experience in the morning we decided to stay on the road and risk meeting German trucks. But after being passed by two German vehicles carrying soldiers, we had a swift change of mind and concluded this was too dangerous. So we went off down a track which led into a steep valley and which seemed to be going in the right direction. Unfortunately the pass was so narrow that after a mile the track rejoined the road. We saw a notice which said 'Passo di Gran Sasso,' which meant we were outflanking the Gran Sasso, the highest mountain in Italy, to the west. Just then a Volkswagen with a German officer rushed past. Another close shave!

The road led down to a small village called Colle through which ran a secondary road. We asked a boy if there were Germans in the village, and he replied '*Si.*' To make sure, we asked a man and he said the same. I thought this would mean us spending the night out; not a pleasant prospect. Then a man leading a mule came past. He asked if we wanted somewhere to sleep. We of course said 'Yes,' so he told us to follow him. We thought he might perhaps be taking us to the Germans, but we were prepared to risk it. We soon reached his house in the middle of a long street through the village. He sat us down in front of the fire and we talked to several of his relatives who came in. We heard the noise of a truck outside in the street, and the man remarked in a casual way '*Le Tedeschi.*' The people were certainly very cool about it. It turned out there was a German headquarters about two hundred yards away.

ASSISTED PASSAGE

That evening we were able to change some of our clothes. Scotty was given a shirt as his was badly torn, and a better jacket. I got a new pair of pants. We were taken to a barn for the night and provided with a sort of eiderdown. This with our blankets made us very warm and for the first time I felt very itchy, of which more later. It had been a good day in spite of our struggle in the snow. We had covered twelve miles and had got away from that bleak village Poggio Cancelli; we now had the Gran Sasso behind us. It was a satisfactory feeling that we were making progress towards our goal, although inevitably we were encountering more Germans.

At 8.30 a.m. next morning 18th November, after a light breakfast in a house near the barn where we had spent the night, we set out guided by an old lady from that house. She amazed us by leading us along back alleys and through gardens, pointing out unconcernedly where the Germans lived, until we left the village and went down through fields and olive groves. After walking for about an hour we came to a point overlooking the road from Armatrice and Pizzoli which divided, one branch going to Aquila, the other to Rieti and Rome. The old lady pointed out our route and then left us. The villagers of Colle whom we met were some of the bravest Italians we encountered in the whole of our walk.

The weather had much improved and we enjoyed the walk in a fine clear morning. What a contrast to twenty four hours before. We reached the top of a shoulder of a mountain, and there laid out before us was the city of Aquila, quite the largest we had seen on our journey. It was pleasant to sit down and watch the scene below us. The roads and the railway were carrying a lot of traffic, German vehicles among them. Presently three Spitfires came over and were engaged by German 88mm anti-aircraft guns.

We were making for Paganica and later for Popoli which is on the Pescara river, the last big river we had to cross. Soon after we set off again, I found a leaflet written in German with a picture of German skeletons looking into the river Dnieper.

84

It was one of our propaganda leaflets describing to Germans soldiers how the war was going against them, particularly in Russia. On the bottom was a note written in Italian asking Italians if they found it to give it to a German soldier.

Later that day we met a Belgian lad and four English soldiers. It seemed there were quite a number of ex-prisoners of war living in the district, including about twenty in Aquila itself. These men said they had been as far as the Pescara, but could not go on as they found the Italians were too frightened to give them food, because of the large number of Germans about. As we neared the village of Tempera only one and a half miles from Paganica, an Italian, who spoke English fairly well having been in America, told us there were Germans in Paganica and they quite often came to Tempera; so it would be risky to go there that night. After some discussion we agreed to go up the hill to an empty house where another four British soldiers lived. They received us very well and let us stay the night. They corroborated the story about the difficulties of going further south. Regarding our route immediately ahead, I was in favour of going along the valley as it was much easier walking. But Scotty and Jack thought the hills were safer. I agreed to go their way and I think they were right.

After dark we went with some of the soldiers down to Tempera where they said we would be able to get a meal. There was a local who they called Johnny who had been very good to them, so we went to his house, but then decided to split up, each of us being taken by one of our lads to a different house. These fellows were so well accepted by the locals it seemed as if they ran the village. They knew nearly everyone, and went in and out of the houses as they liked. If they did not like the look of something cooking in one house, they went to another. A Scots lad took me to a house where I was given two helpings of *minestra*, apples and walnuts. Eventually we forgathered at Johnny's house. He told us that in the morning he would go to Aquila to contact some Communist

ASSISTED PASSAGE

organisation, who could give us introductions to people who could help us through the line. It was all rather vague and I had little hope of this, but we agreed to wait till he returned from Aquila to hear what he had been able to arrange, if anything.

A shave next morning freshened us up, though it was a rather painful business as the blades were getting so blunt. While we were waiting for Johnny to return from Aquila some people from the village brought up some fried potatoes. Presently three soldiers we met yesterday came in. Scotty collected the addresses of all seven. When and if we get through, we would inform their next of kin.

Jack suggested we should abandon our Italian haversacks as they were too conspicuous, and use sacks instead. But these were hard to come by and we only managed to get a small one. This meant that most of our things had to go in Scotty's big sack which was already heavy enough. We got rid of several small articles we thought we could do without. Jack was in favour of discarding our blankets to lighten the load, but I was definitely against this idea as I had visions of us being snowed up for the winter, when we should need them. In fact we were to be very glad of them, as there were some cold nights in front of us.

We found it very difficult to tear ourselves away from the people of Tempera. Johnny had returned to say it would be all right for us to go to Aquila, but was vague about getting introductions which would help us through the line. So we set off about 3.00 p.m., climbing up the hill to leave Paganica on our right. Afterwards we came to a deep ravine up which ran the secondary road from Paganica to Assergi and the Gran Sasso hotel. It was in this hotel that Mussolini was detained after he was removed from power, and from which German paratroops under General Student rescued him. Some considerable time later when we were back in England I met Private Jennings who had been in my Carrier platoon. He told how he was in the vicinity of the Gran Sasso hotel on the day the German paratroops dropped in. He and another man concealed themselves beside the road, and presently were witness to the amazing sight of Mussolini, who was nearly all in with exhaustion, being dragged along by two burly German soldiers, while the officer in charge shouted at Mussolini to go quicker.

That night we reached the village of Pescomaggiori where we went to the priest's house. We talked in front of his diminutive fire for about an hour. We learnt that the province of Abbruzzi in which we were now, lacks extensive woodlands, and consequently timber and firewood are scarce. Therefore the fireplaces are small. Eventually we were taken to the house of the priest's *padroni* or his own particular farmer. There seemed to be about twelve people in his family. The house was bare with the same small fireplace. No Italian house of this type has carpets on the floor, and the only chairs are small and straight backed. One does not see an easy arm chair. That night we slept on a bed of maize leaves and with our blankets and a cover the woman of the house had lent us, we were very warm.

On our walk the next day we met three muleteers who are usually very knowledgeable about tracks leading across country. They warned us not to go to Barisciano as there were Germans there, but to take a route further north through San Stefano and Calascio (pronounced Calash by the people of the district who often omit the last syllable of names). We carried on through the village of San Martino and were making fair progress when an Italian leading a mule passed us. Suddenly realising who we were he shouted *'Tedeschi, tedeschi!'* He was nearly hysterical and said there were two Germans just round the corner. Jack rushed off to the cover of some trees about three hundred yards away and Scotty and I followed. I always got annoyed when we 'flapped' like this, somehow never quite believing what these excitable Italians said. We waited for about a quarter of an hour watching the track. Then up the hill above the track a farmer appeared with his dog and what might have been two Germans in greatcoats.

ASSISTED PASSAGE

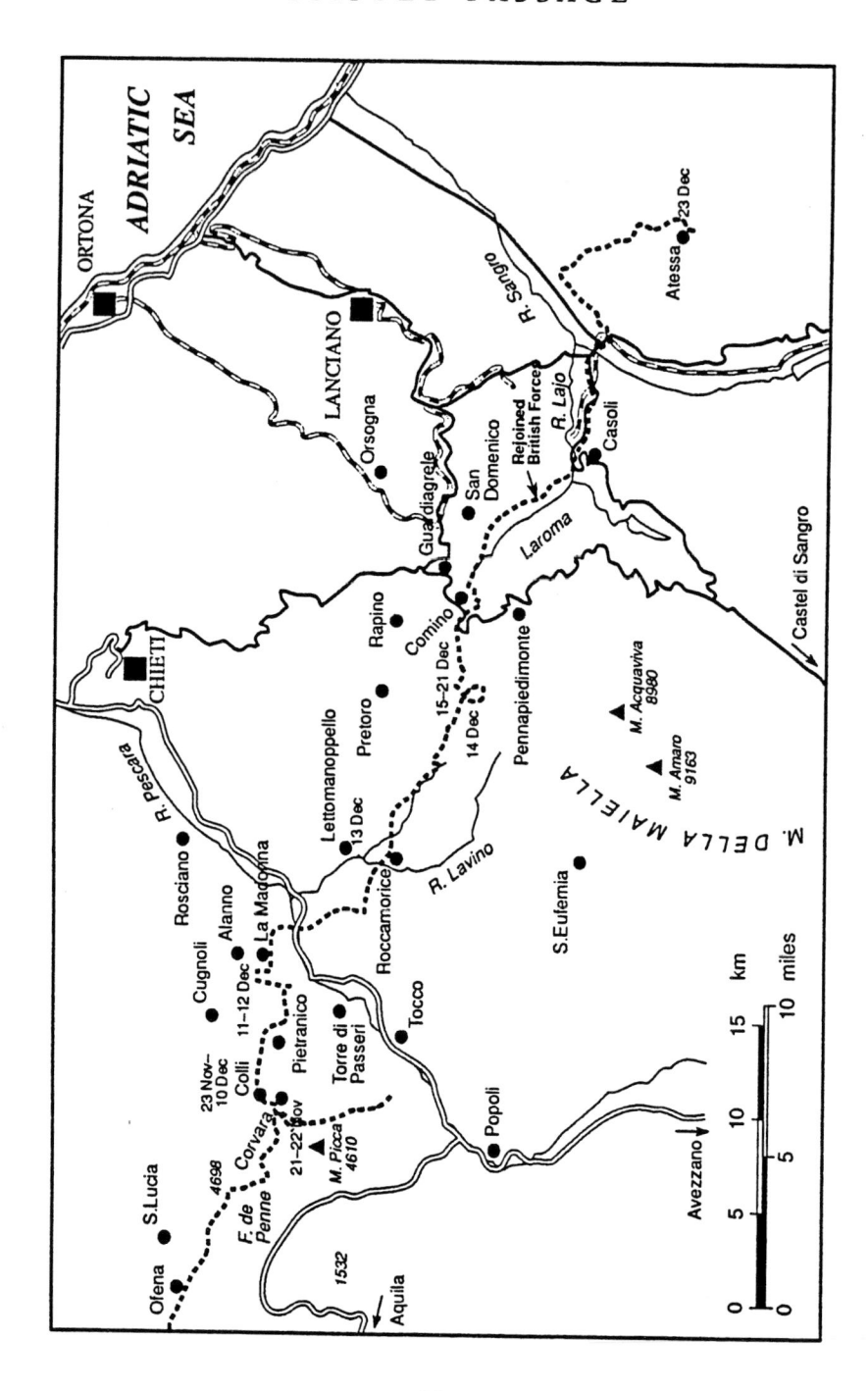

But these looked too blue and we had difficulty in seeing them properly. They seemed to be talking about the sheep and we thought they may have been Germans requisitioning sheep. However they went on and we regained the track after a short detour. As a result of this scare we arranged that one of us went about a hundred yards in front carrying nothing, and the other two carried the large and small sacks. We would change roles periodically.

As we neared San Stefano we had a fine view of the Maiella range. It did not look very far and beyond that were the British. We were undecided whether to go to Calascio or Rocca Calaschio, and finally chose the latter. This meant a very steep climb, longer than we expected. When we reached the top of the ridge there was no sign of the village. So we went along the crest which was 4,800 feet high, past an old castle perched right on top of the hill. Darkness was coming on and we were beginning to give up hope of finding the village, when suddenly I saw a house and there was Rocca Calaschio. It was well named, a mere twelve houses perched on top of the bare and precipitous mountain. Later we discovered that this situation for villages is quite common in Abbruzzi. We were invited into a small house where the family were just about to start their evening meal. We were loath to intrude and said we would eat what we had with us. But they insisted we join them and partake of their *minestra*. It was nice but very peppery hot, which is a custom in Abbruzzi. During the evening they told us that the Germans were stealing sheep, pigs and mules. In Castelvecchio they had burnt down a house because the people had helped the British.

The morning of 21st November broke bright and clear and we made an early start. After about an hour we sat down to have some breakfast and enjoy the marvellous view which lay in front of us. On our left nestling under the lee of the mountain was Castel del Monte where there was a German hospital. To our front was the village of Santa Lucia. Both looked very attractive with smoke from newly lit fires rising from their chimneys. To the south east on low ground lay Popoli and the river Pescara and beyond the majestic Maiella range.

Most of the farms in this area seemed to carry a big head of sheep. We were surprised to find that lambing was at its height and the men were very busy. At one farm we saw a crowd gathered round a cave and we went to investigate. The people were sheep farmers and their families. A number of dead sheep lay about and we saw several wicker baskets holding sheep's milk cheeses. We learnt from one of the men that at this time of the year they normally take their sheep by train to better grazing on the plains near Foggia and Rome. Now they could not do this because of the fighting. This man told us that a big farmer in the district had explained the problem to the local German commander, and asked whether there was any possibility of getting to Foggia. The German said he would arrange it. The farmer must produce his sheep, over a thousand, at the station on a certain day. This the farmer did, and when they were all loaded on the train, the German thanked the farmer for collecting them and said they were now going to Germany! Fifteen to twenty people lived in this cave and they traded wool and cheese for bread and other food.

A long descent over rough ground brought us near the village of Ofena which we passed on our left. The going was treacherous if not dangerous especially for the one carrying the big sack, as we were scrambling and slipping. At San Silvestre an old man told us it would be fatal to go to Popoli. That morning our bombers had damaged a factory there, and German anti-aircraft guns were all round the town. He advised us to go up the mountain on our left and down to the river Pescara at a place called Torre, six miles east of Popoli.

So off we set up the hill again. It was a long, weary climb perhaps because we had little energy. However we eventually reached the pass called Forca di Penne. As we came over the top we saw a new type of country unfolding in front of us. It was undulating with some steep hills, but they were much lower than the mountains we had recently been travelling through. The most striking feature was the number of farms. There were hundreds of them, a welcome change from the sparsely inhabited country we had moved through during the last few days. We surmised that this would be an easier area to live in, though it would almost certainly contain more Germans.

A man on a horse accosted us and asked where we were going, as they all do. He thought we were mad when we told him we intended to cross the Pescara river, and said we must go no farther or we would run into Germans. Another man said the same thing. However we went on and came in sight of the village of Corvara, perched in typically Abbruzzi fashion on a bare rock ridge. We came to a small farm just before the village, and there an old man who could speak some English, having been in Pittsburgh and Philadelphia, asked us into his one roomed house. He said he could not put us up but other families could. Again we were told it was impossible to cross the Pescara as all the bridges were guarded. We were taken to the barn of another house where we spent a cold and rather cramped night.

The next morning the old man offered us some of the potatoes he was boiling. I think he lived on potatoes like the Irish peasants in the last century. His diet seemed to be potatoes with a little bread he baked himself and a few nuts. His main standby was tobacco and he spent what little money he had on that and olive oil. We accompanied him up Monte Picco and then left him. He was sorry to see us go as he was sure we would be recaptured. If we were not retaken, but prevented from going any farther, he said we must come back to Corvara.

Soon afterwards we met a British and a South African soldier and talked to them about the prospects of crossing the river. They surprised us by saying the crossing was easy. They had crossed by a railway bridge west of Tocca. But their problems started once they were south of the river. They reckoned it was almost impossible to live on the far side. There were many Allied and Yugoslav service men hiding there until the British line moved forward; and they had what little food was available. There were Germans in every village. Most of the ex-prisoners were living in caves on the slopes of the Maiella, though there were a few in villages. They reckoned the Germans were constructing a rear line along the river Orte, a fast flowing tributary of the Pescara which flowed through steep banks off the Maiella range. They had great difficulty when trying to get over an eastern shoulder of the range, where several German anti-aircraft guns were sited. Yesterday when going through a wood two English soldiers in front of them were fired on by Germans. With that they decided to turn round, and wait north of the Pescara till the Eighth Army came nearer.

This was a bitter blow to us. We had imagined we were on the last lap and now it seemed we would have to wait. Jack reckoned this was where we stopped until the Army came to us. I could not bring myself to accept this, though I knew in my heart of hearts that it was the right policy in view of the information we had been given. We argued the point for about an hour and a half, but finally agreed to try to time our next advance with a German withdrawal; and if possible to cross the Pescara as the Germans were pulling back over it. At any rate we should wait until the British had taken Chieti.

We had been walking for six weeks and two days from Pessola in Parma province. In the three weeks since leaving Perreto we had done one hundred and ninety three miles.

So we went back to Corvara to the house where we stayed the previous night.

Marking Time

DURING our second night at Corvara I lay awake worrying over our future and trying to look positively on the big disappointment of having to stop walking and stay north of the Pescara till the 8th Army came nearer. How long would this be? Perhaps more to the point, how long would we be allowed to stay in this area? Although there were many farms they were all small and the people were poor. The Germans were obviously in the area in strength and were determined to prevent the Allies crossing the Pescara for as long as possible. This was all part of their defence of Rome, because if Popoli fell the 8th Army would be able to swing left and go for Avezzano and threaten Rome from the east.

However in the morning the outlook seemed brighter. We all thought we would have to wait in this area only for about a week or ten days. It was perhaps just as well we could not visualise the difficulty of mud and terrain facing 8th Army. To cheer ourselves up and plan for the future, we had a long discussion on our best route south. The big obstacle was the Maiella range. It was virtually impossible to cross in mid winter with its heavy covering of snow. Consequently we could go either to the right or west of it by Popoli to Sulmona and then over the narrow, steep pass to Castel di Sangro, which we heard, mistakenly, the British had just taken. Alternatively we could keep to lower ground east of the Maiella, probably between Guardiagrele and the sea. But this was of course where the main part of the German army was in position. We decided the latter was the better of two not very attractive alternatives. However we hoped to keep as near the lower slopes of the Maiella as possible, as we thought the Germans would not be so thick on the ground in that part of their defences.

Our days in the Corvara and Colli area developed into a sort of routine. We would move round contacting the Allied soldiers whom we got to know fairly well. One was a Trooper in 4 Hussars who had been captured in Greece. He had been in a prison camp at Aquila and was now working on a farm and the people were feeding him. From him we heard of and later met a Trooper Cliff, 4 Royal Tank Regiment. He had been in the area for a month and was also working on a farm. He knew a student who spoke reasonable English and who went to Corvara in the evenings to listen to the News on the radio. Other Allied nationals we encountered were two Americans, three South Africans and two Englishmen. They had been in the area for three weeks and they thought it safer to go up the mountain each night and sleep in the woods. The Americans confirmed, and in fact amplified, what we had heard about conditions the other side of the Pescara river. Two others were a R.A.M.C. corporal who came from Sheriff Hill, Co. Durham and who had been captured in the Gazala fighting. With him was a big tall man in the Essex Regiment who had been taken in the early stages of the fighting at El Alamein. He said he had been billeted in Northumberland for a long time, and the people were the most hospitable he had met. They had been in Macerata Camp and when they got out they joined a Partisan band near Ascoli for a short time. They had been involved in quite a successful battle with the Germans. There were several other Allied nationals living in the area and apart from doing some work on farms, they spent their days much as we did.

Frequently we climbed up from Corvara or Colli to Monte Picco. We did this because it was out of the way of visiting Germans, and on a clear day one could see signs of the battle in the distance. We always tried to decide whether the signs were nearer or not. We usually met some British and South African lads there. Near the top of Monte Picco was a fairly large white house in which four Italian officers lived. They frequently heard the News and they became about our best source of information. We discovered their mood and their welcome to us or anyone else was in direct relation to how good the news was. If the British were advancing or had captured a town, they were very friendly. On the other hand if it was obvious the Germans had counter attacked or the Allies were making no progress, they were surly and off hand, and made derogatory remarks about the British army.

Apart from food and shelter the most important thing in our lives was the news. Several people listened to the Italian broadcasts and occasionally one heard an English bulletin. But the news we got was usually second or third hand, and it was difficult to separate facts from wishful thinking. Then in addition rumours abounded and travelled fast. For example we heard that the 8th Army had captured Lanciano and were advancing on Ortona. Two days later they were still fighting for Lanciano. Then we were told they had taken Orsogna and Guardiagrele. Had this been true it would have made our task much easier. We thought this was premature, particularly in respect of Guardiagrele, and we were right. The only certainty was that the Germans in their usual efficient way were fighting a dogged defensive battle, considerably aided by the nature of the country and the very wet weather. We were frequently soaked as we moved from one house or shelter to another. Now the days as well as the nights were cold, so we often felt pretty miserable. However we usually managed to dry out in the evenings in spite of the small fires in Abbruzzi farmhouses.

The signs of battle cheered us up, particularly the demonstrations of Allied air power. We saw mainly Spitfires and Warhawks performing as fighter bombers. One afternoon we had a splendid view of our medium bombers pounding Pescara and the bridges over the river there. Several tremendous flashes were followed by columns of smoke and dust rising many hundred feet in the air. The German anti-aircraft fire was intense as the 88mm guns around Pescara, Chieti and near Rosciano engaged the bombers. But we never saw a plane shot down. Once or twice we were in the Italian officers' house when an air raid started. They would rush out to get a good view shouting 'Montgomery! Montgomery!'

On 27th November we were coming down from Monte Picco and had just got to the unfinished road above Colli, when we met a man leading a mule and got into conservation with him. He told us he would show us a place to sleep that night. He led us to a small barn standing by itself at the edge of the road. Here we dumped our sacks and saw there was some quite good straw in the barn and altogether it looked a promising place. Our only worry was that it was rather close to the road. The man then took us along to his house, where his wife was making *polenta* in a small bare room with a flagged stone floor and very little furniture. There was a good fire over which she was vigorously stirring a big boiling pot. When it was cooked she wiped the table with a rag and tipped the *polenta* on to it. It ran over the table like lava from a volcano. It set quickly and she then put tomato purée and a little grated cheese over it. Whereupon everyone collected round the table and set to, sharing the three forks between us. It certainly saved washing up plates! The *polenta* was quite nice and there was plenty for everybody. It is filling and one cannot eat very much of it. We had heard of this communal eating of *polenta*, but this was the first time we had seen it.

On 29th November we decided to do a reconnaissance towards the river Pescara to see if we could find any likely crossing points. We followed a track between the village of Pietranico and a bare precipitous ridge called La Queglia. Here we met two soldiers who had been batmen in Campo 49 at Fontanellato, and we had a long and interesting talk with them about our respective journeys and experiences. Afterwards we went down another two miles through olive groves and small stony fields. Here we obtained a clear view of the main road from Pescara to Tocco and Popoli. Below was the village of Torre di Passeri. A lot of German transport was moving in both directions on the main road along the valley. We decided not to go any further towards the river as it was already getting dark.

The next day we were sitting eating some bread, cheese and figs which we were carrying in our sacks, when Scotty found a louse on him. Further searching produced several more. Soon Jack and I discovered we were in the same condition. We were absolutely appalled. We thought we must have picked them up either from the straw on which we had been lying in various places, or that the clothes we had changed into at Sechiano on 4th November were already infested. Perhaps it was the clothes we had been given at Colle on 17th November. That was the first time I had felt itchy. Our skins were now very irritable. Two days later we managed to have a bathe in a swiftly running stream. It was quite the coldest bath I have ever had and it took us an hour to get warm again. However we felt cleaner, though I am sorry to say it did not get rid of the lice.

We were at one small farm house at the time of the weekly baking of bread. The woman of the house kneaded the dough. She then cleaned out the oven, which as usual in these parts, was outside the house. She next collected a big bundle of faggots and put them in the oven. These were lit and more were added when the first lot were burnt up. She seemed to know exactly when the oven was hot enough. All the bread, about fifteen loaves, was put in at once. We were allowed to taste a little of the resulting baking, and it was delicious.

I was getting increasingly worried about our security. The fairly large number of British and South African servicemen, together with one or two Americans and Yugoslavs, living in the area must sooner or later come to the notice of the Germans. If they decided to sweep the area, there was a strong possibility we would all be recaptured, and fierce reprisals would be taken against the Italians who were sheltering and feeding us. This thought, coupled with the tedious waiting for the British army to come nearer, which was already longer than we had anticipated; and the wet and cold weather made me and indeed all three of us feel depressed. One had to think that our circumstances might be much worse, and give thanks for what blessings we had. It was on one such day when our morale was low that Scotty and I started to talk about our college days, pre-war club rugger and the people we both knew from those days. I found this most diverting and enabled me to forget for the moment our present circumstances.

During these days we fed in a number of houses in this small area and slept in their barns and cowsheds. One house we frequented more than others belonged to a man called Jovani. He had a large family of five sons and four daughters varying in age from nineteen to one year. Whenever we returned after two or three days elsewhere Jovani always seemed pleased to see us. He usually insisted on us drinking wine with the light breakfast of bread and dripping or beans and potatoes we were given. To my mind it was like drinking beer for breakfast; but the Italians drink wine at any time of the day or night, and we did not want to disappoint him. Towards the end of our time in this valley we received offers of other places to sleep, but we usually returned to Jovani's as we were well 'dug in' there.

On a walk up to Monte Picco on 4th December we had a long talk to the English lads who spend the days in a cave near the top of the mountain. They come down to a barn at night. While we were there, it started to snow and soon the ground had a good covering. This worried us because it was our main fear that we would become snowed up before we could get through the lines. After our experience at Poggio Cancelli we did not want any more snow. Happily it was not a heavy fall and it soon cleared again.

That afternoon we went down to talk to the Italian officers and found them in a much better mood than when we had last seen them. This was because the news was better. They said the British had now secured Lanciano and were pushing on to

Orsogna. Jack could now speak Italian fairly well and he was on easy terms with them. Scotty and I could just about make ourselves understood on a few subjects such as food, English life, America and our prison camp. This may sound quite impressive, but it was the subjects we were questioned on at nearly every house we went into. We did not realise how bad our Italian was until we heard Italians who had been to America a long time ago, trying to speak English. One of the Italians had a pocket chess set and I watched two of them playing. I was then asked to play the winner. Although I had not played since June 1941 during the voyage to the Middle East, my opponent was not very good and I managed to win.

We were about to leave when the Italians asked us to stay to watch pasta being made in the proper Italian manner, and afterwards partake of it. It was fascinating to watch the dough being made and kneaded into the right consistency and then cut up into small strips. It took quite a long time for this meal to be prepared, but it was well worth waiting for.

With so much time on our hands, the three of us often became involved in long complex discussions on a variety of subjects. One I remember was the performance of the British army and the handling of the Armistice. Jack and Scotty reckoned that the slowness of the advance up Italy was due to the miscalculation and mismanagement of the Higher Command. While I agreed about the Armistice, I pointed out the difficulty of the terrain which lent itself to the defence, and also to the unusually wet weather of the last month.

Scotty began to feel poorly on the 8th December. After Trooper Cliff cut our hair which was badly needed, he went back to Jovani's to lie down in the straw, as he was shivery and aching all over. Jack and I discussed the advisability of moving off from this area and trying to cross the Pescara river. He had become as disgruntled as I was at this enforced hanging about, which was now well over our original estimate of a week to ten days. We agreed that if the rumour that we had captured Guardiagrele was correct, we would attempt to get through.

We decided to wait a day or two to make certain of this before we left.

We heard a disturbing story the next day from an English soldier. The night before, he woke up hearing a commotion in the house in which he was sleeping. He jumped out of a window just as a German came in the door. Apparently he had been given away by a local Fascist. The Germans went to two other farms, but did not catch any British men. The Germans were offering a reward of the equivalent of £20 to anyone who was the cause of an Allied soldier being recaptured. We thought £20 a bit of an insult! But we had also heard that the Germans sometimes sent the Fascists away 'with a flea in their ear' when they tried to collect their reward. If the Germans were convinced the information was correct, they would mount a raid. This news strengthened my conviction that we should move off and try to get through the line.

This was confirmed in all our minds on the night of 11th December. At about 3.45 a.m. I was awakened by Jack, who was in the middle, sitting upright. Scotty and I asked him what was the matter and he said 'Didn't you hear that shot?' All the dogs in the neighbourhood were barking, but I did not take much notice. A few minutes later there was another shot, and it was obvious something was afoot. We could hear Jovani and his eldest son talking outside. Jack went out to find out what the trouble was. Jovani told him that having heard two shots and all the dogs barking it must be the Germans, and he had sent his son to find out. While Jack was giving Scotty and I this information, Jovani's wife came in considerably perturbed and wringing her hands and talking about the *'Tedeschi.'* We decided to put our boots on and pack up our blankets.

We then went back into the house. Naturally the whole family was in a high state of excitement and fear. Presently the eldest son—Michele—came back and said the Germans were searching the houses up towards Colli. This family had been extremely good to us and the last thing we wanted was to get them into trouble. So we agreed to leave there and then, taking our sacks with us. There were short farewells; I think they were relieved to see us go. It was raining steadily when we set off, so we decided to go down the valley and wait in one of the huts till daybreak. We found the hut without difficulty. It was damp and cold inside, so we put our blankets round us and made the best of it till dawn. The barking and general excitement seemed to die down after an hour or so, though we heard one more shot.

As it got light we approached the house where the 4 Hussar man lived, but found he had gone. Two women were wringing their hands in a distressed state and looking up towards Corvara. Later we saw twenty Germans scrambling up the rocky La Queglia ridge, pursuing a man who was trying to get away. The Germans were doing a lot of shooting and we heard they had caught some Italian refugees who were living in an empty house in Corvara, but they had not caught any Allied servicemen. Thereupon we decided not to stay any longer in this area. We moved east, climbing a ridge till we were out of sight of Colli and Corvara. That was the last we saw of the Corvara valley where we had been living since the 21st November.

Our appreciation was that it would take three days to get through the line once we had crossed the Pescara river. This was to prove a large underestimate. We thought it would be very difficult to get food south of the river. Therefore we had to conserve and build up our stocks of food in a form which would be light enough to carry easily.

Having crossed the ridge our route lay down a valley. Near the bottom we met a R.A.F. sergeant, who told us he had been one of the crew of a plane which took General Carton de Wiart to the Middle East early in 1941. The plane developed engine trouble and they had to land in the sea near Benghazi. So they were all taken prisoner. The sergeant was also trying to get through, so he came along with us for a time.

We crossed a series of small ridges and over a secondary road which led to the village of Cugnoli. After all the rain the fields in the valley bottoms were very wet and for a time we were walking through liquid mud which was slow and tiring. At the top of the next ridge we recognised the ground having been this way on 3rd December. Pietranico was a little way to the south of us as we crossed the Pietranco to Alanno road, having made sure there were no Germans about. The going was now much easier as we reached flat ground which ran down to the river bank. As we were leaving a wood we met a South African and three English soldiers. With them was an old Italian who had only one eye. They thought we could cross the river without too much difficulty, as about a fortnight before an English officer and a girl had crossed safely. These soldiers lived in a hut in the wood by day and at night slept in a thatched barn. A local girl brought them food each day. Presently she arrived with some food. As there seemed plenty for everyone, we accepted their invitation to go to their hut to eat it.

It was now about 4.00 p.m. and the rain had started again. So we decided to stay north of the river that night and cross in the morning. Whereupon the old man offered to show us a place where we could sleep. We left the four soldiers and followed the old man up a steep hillside. He was amazingly agile practically running up the steep slopes, while we panted and struggled to keep up with him. He took us north for about two and a half miles, crossing the Pietranico–Alanno road again, to the village of La Madonna. We were led into a house on the outskirts of the village, and having tried to scrape some of the mud off our boots, were taken upstairs to a small room. Here was a young man who was a tenant of the one-eyed Italian and he made up a big fire. They gave us a slice of newly baked bread on which was olive oil and salt.

After about an hour or so, the old man took us off over a ploughed field to his own house. We had to wait about a hundred yards away while he went to see that the coast was clear. He came back and led us to his cowshed, which was adjoining the house which stood on the edge of the Pietranico to Alanno road. There was some good straw to sleep on, so we got down to it. I was on the outside next to a big white cow. When eventually I dropped off to sleep, I was woken by a hot draught of air and a slushing noise in my ear. I then realised the cow was chewing the cud about an inch from my face. The cowshed became very hot and I got up and opened the door slightly. Outside I saw a German in the road. Presently two went past talking, and then two more very drunk, having an argument. Several German trucks came past too.

We were woken the next morning by the old man and another bringing in fodder for the cows. I mentioned that I had seen the Germans in the night and he was not surprised. He appeared not to be afraid of the Germans. We came to the conclusion that he, and the people we met at Colle on 17th November, were the best of any on our journey for their lack of fear of the Germans.

We were very disappointed to see it was raining in torrents and we did not think we should go on till it cleared. The old farmer thought it would rain all day. So he took us up to a large barn standing by itself overlooking the Pietranico-Alanno road. We cleared some space of farm implements, tiles and junk and made a fire. It was four days since our last shave, so we took it in turns to scrape our faces. Scotty had never shaken off the flu which he had during the last few days in the Corvara valley, and he was again feeling achy with a headache and a sore throat. We discussed how we should cross the river. We had been told there was a dam and lock over which one could walk, apparently unguarded. The R.A.F. sergeant did not trust this information and decided to go on on his own to try to cross higher up the river.

The rain continued, so we stayed in the barn all day feeling cold and miserable. We watched three German trucks hidden under some trees just off the road below us.

We had been invited to go down to the old farmer's house when it got dark. As we neared the house another man came out and took us into the cowshed, asking us to wait until a visitor had left. After about half an hour the visitor departed, and we were taken into the house and given an excellent meal of *pasta ascuita*, wine and bread. It was about the nicest pasta I had tasted. Poor Scotty was not hungry and could eat very little. We had another night in the cowshed, and apart from the noise of Germans passing on the road outside, I was able to sleep quite well. But before I did, I could not help marvelling at the bravery and generous hospitality of these small Italian farmers. I contemplated the horror of us being responsible for these good people being shot or sent to a concentration camp, and their house burnt down for sheltering Allied soldiers. We would be the lucky ones; we would merely be sent to a Prisoner of War camp in Germany.

In the Shadow of the Maiella

THE next morning 13th December the weather had improved, so we set off for the river Pescara. We left our two smaller blankets in the house, keeping the large one, as we thought we might look suspicious carrying heavy sacks south of the river. Soon after starting an old woman gave us each a large slice of bread. After a short climb over a ridge called La Corte della Plaja, we could see the dam and the sluice gates, and on the far side the railway along which ran an occasional train, and the main road busy with German transport. We sat down on the edge of an oak wood to plan our route. Fortunately we could see a number of culverts under the railway and the road, thus we could avoid having to expose ourselves by going over the top of the embankments on which these main arteries were built. There was a constant stream of German transport moving both ways along the road—staff cars, motor cycles, lorries and even a few horse drawn wagons. Jack said he was in favour of waiting till darkness hid our crossing, but I wanted to have a go straight away. After some discussion we agreed to do this.

The way led down over steep fields past a farm, till we came to within two hundred yards of the houses round the dam. We had been told that in one of these there lived a man who could speak English fairly well, being one of the many Italians who had lived in America for a time.

Jack went on to find this man while Scotty and I waited out of sight. After half an hour and no sign of Jack we began to get worried. But a little later he appeared and signalled us down. The man had told him there was no difficulty in getting across and many people had done it. A carabinieri lived in a house at this end of the dam but he did not usually bother anybody. The best plan was for one to get across and under the road before the next one went. So we agreed that Jack should go first, me second and Scotty last. The Italian gave us a glass of wine, also bread and figs which were welcome as they were easily carried. He said he had been a professional gambler in America and had made a lot of money.

Shortly after twelve noon Jack went across and under the railway and road without mishap. I followed climbing up to the concrete ledge of the dam on which handrails were placed, past the tall tower and the electrical power station. I was surprised at the large size and width of the dam, and noticed that the river was much wider than I had expected. It made one realise what a major obstacle this river would be to the 8th Army. I tried not to hurry and to appear normal to the Germans passing along the main road to whom I was in full view. Having crossed the dam, I passed a group of men working near the railway. They looked at me rather suspiciously and asked if I was *'Slavi'* or *'Inglesi?'* I took no notice, followed a path left, went under the railway and road and climbed up an open field beyond. Again I felt very exposed to the prying German eyes travelling along the road. Scotty followed me quite successfully. So after all the stories about the difficulties, if not impossibility, of crossing the Pescara river, we had done it without any trouble. Apart from getting through the actual line itself, this had been our main objective for several weeks. It was with a feeling of great relief that we set off again towards our last and most important goal.

We struck a good path leading steadily uphill. Soon we had to make a careful crossing of a secondary road, which led off the main Pescara to Popoli route up to the village of San Eufemia, which lay to the west of the Maiella range some miles to the south. German trucks and halftracks were using this road, but we were able to cross it without trouble. When going over a small ravine, my left boot which had a big hole in the uppers, became filled with mud. We had to stop while

I emptied it. I wondered how much longer by boots were going to be wearable. We avoided houses and farms as much as we could, as we climbed higher all the time. Fairly late in the afternoon we met two Italians who said there were many Germans in the area, but they did not seem frightened at the thought. Two women told us that a fairly large number of English and Allied ex-prisoners had been retaken by the Germans in this area.

As the afternoon wore on we began to look for empty barns or sheep huts where we might sleep. We then had to cross the river Lavino which ran through a deep, wide gorge. It took us a long time to do this. To the south of us lay the village of Roccamorice in which there was a company of Germans. There was nothing strange in that, as the Italians said they were in every village between the Pescara and the front line. We asked two girls if there was a barn in which we could spend the night, but they did not know of one. After a lot of hanging about Jack and I found a barn about a quarter of a mile away. We saw the owner and he had no objection to us sleeping there. When we returned from the barn we found Scotty in a little cottage where two women were cooking a meal for us. This was a pleasant surprise, as we had imagined that once across the Pescara we would have to fend for ourselves. It proved to be the last meal we had in an Italian farm house.

We left the house about 8.30 p.m. and went to bed in our barn. The moon was full and it was a lovely night. Now we had only the one big blanket which only just covered us. There was not much straw to lie on, and I spent a cold and restless night, wondering what the morrow would bring. Nevertheless we had the satisfaction of knowing we had crossed the Pescara and made good progress towards the line.

We rose at dawn and saw that thick mist was down on the mountains. We discovered that most of the figs we had been carrying had fallen into the straw. Though we found a few, most of them were lost. This was a blow as they were a valued part of our rations. As we crossed a ravine carrying the river

San Angelo the mist cleared. We could hear some German singing and presently saw a company marching out from Lettomanopello, a large village to the north of us. We struck a path leading up the mountain. We had been warned this path was occasionally used by German patrols, so we were particularly on the look out. The path led ever upward and later became very steep. Our pace got slower the higher we went. I think this was the longest and steepest climb in the whole of our journey.

At last we reached a plateau called Piano di Tarica and entered some beech woods, at the end of which was an upland pasture. Two old men who came from Pretoro were tending sheep grazing the pasture. Just then the mist cleared temporarily and we got a fleeting glimpse of Guardiagrele, which the man said was still held by the Germans. When we told them we were aiming to get through the line, they said we were mad as it was quite impossible.

We soon got cold standing talking to the shepherds; so having obtained as much information as we could, we set off again keeping to the high ground. Presently we came across several men cutting down trees and collecting wood, which they loaded on to mules and on to each others' backs. It was amazing how much they could carry. On our left was a prominent track leading from Pretoro up into Monte Maiella, and which apparently the Germans used to supply their garrison of Alpine troops on the mountain. We had decided from what we had been told and from the not very good map we had with us, that our best way led due east. But the tracks we were on were taking us south. So we cut off to the left into a wood where we were hampered by large rocks and thick undergrowth. Suddenly we came upon a road, which we agreed must be the one up from Pretoro. The Germans had widened and resurfaced it. We were debating whether to cross it when we heard a truck approaching. We were in the open so all we could do was to lie down flat on our faces; and the truck which was full of Germans, went past.

The ground started to rise again. Because the mist had come down thickly again we were not certain of where we were. Next we were faced with a tremendous gorge. Our only method of progression was to go running and slipping down, hanging on to branches and anything that would hold us. The one carrying the sack had only one hand to hang on with. To our great relief we struck a small track, but we had not been going along this very far when we heard voices. Then I saw a German carrying a log and another near a small pumping plant. This was rather discouraging—we were meeting Germans everywhere.

So we had no alternative to leaving the path, going down a short way, over a stream and up the steep and almost heartbreaking climb the other side. On reaching the top we hit another small path. Going direct through the wood was so difficult, we decided to follow this. We were progressing well along the path till we came round a bend, and there, about forty yards away was a German with a sub machine gun. Luckily he did not see us, so we went into the trees and began to descend another steep ravine. Again we slipped and scrambled our way to the bottom. We stood under a big rock out of the rain which had started, and ate some bread and cheese, with the stream rushing past our feet. As we ate we felt cold, wet and miserable, lost in an unknown world of woods and ravines. However when we started off again climbing the almost vertical side of the gorge we soon got warm and we felt we were getting somewhere, even if we did not know where.

It was now getting late and the light was beginning to go, and we had no idea where we were going to spend the night. The wood began to thin out and we looked for a hut. After half an hour just as we were coming to the conclusion we would have to sleep out, Jack found one. It was a hut used by the shepherds in summer. We blocked up one end, cleared out the inside and unsuccessfully tried to light a fire. So we settled ourselves for the night. But we were cramped and cold, so did not sleep much. The walking that day had undoubtedly been the worst we had ever had. But we were cheered by the sounds of battle which seemed quite close.

We woke next morning to find ourselves still shrouded in thick mist. Having eaten a slice of bread and a few figs each, we set off thinking this would be our last day's walking. We went through beech woods on a rough compass bearing of south east. We came across a man collecting charcoal from a flat platform-like place where charcoal burners had been working. He did not look like a German, so we asked him the best way towards Guardiagrele. Though rather surly and unfriendly, he told us to go down, cross a ravine and hit a path on the other side. We came to the edge of this ravine a few yards farther on. All we could see was that the ground fell away very steeply into what looked like a great misty abyss. After yesterday's experiences with these frightful steep sided ravines, we were loath to tackle this one. However there seemed to be no way round it, so down we went, hanging on to the trees, rocks or anything which came to hand to stop one falling. We eventually reached the stream at the bottom where we had an enjoyable drink from the cool clear water. The mist lifted for a few minutes and we could see tracks leading up the other side of the ravine, along one of which a man and a woman with a mule were going. We were surprised to see Italians so near the battle and supposed they must be refugees from one of the villages lower down.

There were a number of paths leading off the one we were on and we were undecided which one to take. After a stiff climb we came to a wider path which seemed to follow the direction of the valley. The mist had now come down again thicker than ever, and it was becoming obvious we were pretty well lost. The track seemed to lead on interminably as we crossed several streams cascading down the mountain. Then we stumbled on a hut similar to the one we were in last night. Two men were outside it, with an old man inside lying on a couch. We learnt that four men live in this hut and the women of the family who live in Rapino, occasionally bring up food for the men. They gave us a little bread and cheese, and in exchange Scotty gave them some leaf tobacco he had been given at the house near Alanno. The Italians said they knew where some British officers were living fairly near by. So we persuaded them to show us, as no amount of directions would have been any good in this thick mist.

We were led along the track we had been on that morning. Then to our great surprise we came to the place where we had spoken to the man who was collecting charcoal. Evidently we had been going round in a circle, confirming that we were completely lost. In a brief thinning of the mist, the Italians pointed out the track we must follow, as it gradually descended to lower ground. We now made better progress. As we came to another of these mountain huts, a man passed us who I thought was a German. Jack and I ignored him, but we turned round to see Scotty talking to him. He was a small, sallow, rat of a man who we learned was a German deserter. He kept repeating *'Hitler kaput.'* He was very nervous and seemed morally shattered.

Presently we came across some people standing round a dismembered cow. Apparently they had killed it shortly before it was going to die of tuberculosis. In this group was a soldier from the Rifle Brigade. He took us to a small cave-like place where an English officer and an English girl lived. We thought they must be the two we had heard about shortly before we crossed the Pescara river. But they were not there. So he took us to another cave where two officers were living. They were even more dirty and dishevelled than we were, and were extremely rude and did not want to talk to us. Apparently they used the German deserter, who had been in charge of artillery horses near Rapino until he had had enough and deserted, to collect charcoal and run errands for them. I thought this arrangement foolishly dangerous. However one of these two showed us a very low stone structure where we might spend the night. One had to crawl through the entrance and inside there was just enough room to sit up.

There was a little charcoal in the shelter, so Jack fetched a glowing piece from the officer and girl's hut. We put this amongst our charcoal and started blowing, taking it in turns as it was exhausting work. After about three quarters of an hour we got a small fire going. Just before we went to bed we heard voices approaching up the path which ran outside the shelter. They turned out to be the English officer and the girl. After a short chat we agreed to meet in the morning. We then tried to settle ourselves for the night. There was just room for the three of us to lie stretched out, two heads at one end and one at the other.

I was feeling very cold as we crawled out of the little shelter in the morning. Having folded the blanket we ate a slice of bread and three figs each. We rationed ourselves to this amount, though by now we were very hungry.

Presently the English officer we had met last night came over and introduced himself as Douglas De Cent. He was a Lieutenant in the Kent Yeomanry Field Regiment Royal Artillery. He had been in camp at Sulmona and was later moved to Bologna. He knew Ian Pitt from 8 D.L.I., but thought that Ian had not got away from Chieti camp. De Cent had been walking with Dick Ellis, a Flight Lt. in the R.A.F. who had been at school at Oundle with me. About six weeks before, they had met a Yugoslav and the English girl. Soon after reaching this place about three weeks before, the Yugoslav had disappeared and Dick Ellis had gone on his own. But there was no news about what had happened to him.

Though the Maiella range was still shrouded in mist, the sun shone on the lower ground. Douglas pointed out the main features of the country over which the battle was now being fought. The track we were on led down to the village of Rapino. At the moment civilians were still living in it. Round the village were several German artillery positions and we could see their guns firing. Slightly to the right was Guardiagrele standing up prominently on a steep ridge along which ran a road to Penne Piedimonte which was just out of sight to the south west. To the north east of Guardiagrele was Orsogna, which had changed hands more than once, but at the moment was held by the Germans. Beyond in the distance just visible in the haze was Ortona on the coast, which the Canadians were attacking. We could also see Lanciano which the British had held for about a fortnight. We were amazed to see the great difficulties the ground imposed on the attacking troops, and conversely how it aided the defence. The ridges were steep, the roads few and their quality bad. There were no less than four ridges between the present position of the 8th Army, which we could roughly discern, and Chieti—the key to the Pescara valley. Incidentally we could also see the steep valley or ravine in which we became involved yesterday. It ran down nearly to Rapino.

Although we did not know it at the time, what we were looking at was the German Gustav line, their main winter position and the strongest river line in Italy. It ran from the coast, where the 8th Army had succeeded in breaking into it, to Orsogna and Guardiagrele, then down to Castel di Sangro and across to the river Rapido and Cassino and on to the river Garigliano which ran into the sea on the west coast.

Douglas was a fairly tall, slim fresh faced man. He was agreeable and easy to get on with. Sometimes he showed he had difficulty in coming to a decision. This perhaps was because he felt in a protective capacity to his girl companion, for whom he felt a strong affection. But when we teamed up with them, Douglas was always entirely reliable.

Douglas said he, like us, was keen to try to get through the lines, but was held back by the risk of taking a girl with him. He had heard that about ten days before, a party of a dozen British ex-prisoners led by two Paratroop officers had attempted to get through but had been intercepted, and the rumour was that two had been shot. So he was nervous of exposing themselves to danger of that sort. They had therefore decided to stay till our troops had captured Guardiagrele, which Douglas thought would be in the next week. The other possibility was to be smuggled through among a crowd of civilians who, it was rumoured, were occasionally allowed to go through the German lines on their way further south. I personally did not set much store by that story. Therefore a more or less conscious decision was taken, that we should remain in this area for a few days until either Guardiagrele fell or we could get through among a bunch of civilians. This of course could all be altered if the food ran out, in which case we would have to make the attempt or go back north of the Pescara. That to me at that particular time was unthinkable.

After this interesting conversation, Douglas took us over to his cave to meet the girl whose name was Gillian Weatherall. She seemed very nice, down to earth, practical and more than willing to pull her weight. She had been married to an Italian doctor and lived in Florence. She had been arrested by the Italian police for allegedly helping British prisoners of war. After a grim three months in prison, she had been sent to Macerata internment camp. Shortly after the Armistice she had managed to get away from there and went up into the hills, as we had. She spoke fluent Italian, which in the present situation was very useful as she could go down to Rapino to collect food, and be better accepted by the local people than perhaps we might. Consequently they were doing fairly well for food at that moment. Douglas and Gillian were friendly and generous to us at a time when they had difficulties of their own. They agreed to us joining them, gave us a little meat, beans and a few potatoes, and lent us an old casserole dish in which to cook a stew.

We found that the preparation of this meal took us about three hours, because of the difficulty of getting the charcoal fire hot enough to boil the stew, and to keep it there for the two hours needed to soften the meat and the beans. However when at last it was cooked we really enjoyed it, as we were very hungry. We had only two spoons so we passed them round, taking it in turns to be the one without. During the next few days Scotty did most of the cooking.

Afterwards we went up to a spring from which everyone in this area got their water. We had a cold but satisfactory wash at the spring. We had been told that four English soldiers were living in a cave near our shelter, so Jack and I went to meet them. We found the cave in a well concealed position, difficult of access down a steep path over the edge of a ravine, and hidden by a screen of fir trees. These lads had been in the camp at Sulmona and had lived in this cave for a month, partly because one of them had a septic leg and could not walk. Their plan was to wait until the British troops arrived.

Back at the shelter we tried to get a charcoal fire going. By means of prolonged blowing we managed to warm the shelter a little. Charcoal was the only fuel we could use, because the smoke from a wood fire would make the shelter uninhabitable. We fell to discussing our present situation and future plans. We really needed much better information about the layout of the German and British positions, if we were to attempt to get through in the immediate future. The persistent mist and low cloud were a considerable hindrance. If we were to stay until the British had captured Guardiagrele, as we had agreed with Douglas and Gillian, our main problem, apart from avoiding the Germans, was food. That day we had been able to buy some meat for forty lira from a farmer. Tough and poor though it was, any food was welcome. We realised that for the first time on our journey we were going to have to buy food. We could not complain at this, as the Italians were short of food themselves. I now discovered I had left a hundred lira note in my battle dress trousers which I exchanged at Sechiana on 4th November. Scotty and Jack were very nice about it, but I cursed myself for a fool, because we were now going to need that money.

Consequently during the next few days our main occupation was hunting for food and something to cook it in, as we did not want to have to borrow Douglas and Gillian's pot all the time. Ironically after never being without bread on our journey, bread was now the food we most desired and were short of. During this searching we came across families of shepherds living in the woods, with their sheep penned nearby. They dared not let them out for fear of the Germans stealing them. Other families were living in caves or huts in the side of the gorge, keeping their mules in other caves. We were unsuccessful in our requests for food from all these people.

The next day, after our usual breakfast of half a slice of bread and three figs each, I went on a reconnaissance with Gillian to see the route taken by a party attempting to take cattle through the line. Going down the track leading to Rapino, then right handed across the Aquafreddo stream, we came to a grassy plateau where we hoped to get a view of the country to the east. As we arrived there we saw a group of Germans walking along very sloppily with hands in pockets and some not wearing hats. I thought they might be deserters, but they were carrying rifles. After they had gone, we caught only a short glimpse of Guardiagrele before the mist came down again. On the way back across some fields we saw all the sheep being collected together. As we watched we realised it was the Germans who were gathering them. They drove off about fifteen hundred sheep and twelve mules, thus removing completely the livelihood of the shepherds and their families. Later Jack and I nearly ran into a German officer and a soldier who were talking to an Italian who lived in a hut just above Douglas's shelter. Jack mumbled something in Italian, and we went off down the path past our own shelter, trying to look natural. As we were hiding in some fir trees, the German deserter came up. He was frightened out of his wits, because he knew if he was caught he would be shot. But we did not want him anywhere near us, and told him so in no uncertain terms. That evening we discussed the situation with Gillian and Douglas, and agreed that this immediate vicinity is being visited too often by Germans. So we decided that the five of us would move up the mountain to two huts made of fir trees near the place where we get charcoal.

The next morning Jack went on ahead to reserve at least one of the huts in case others had had the same idea. Scotty and I joined him after filling our water bottles at the spring. Jack had seen four Germans going down a track just below him. The German deserter, who had been collecting charcoal, was hiding behind Jack absolutely shivering with fright. The four Germans came back up the path on their way to their hut above the snow line on the Maiella. They were Alpine troops.

Sketch from memory of a hut on the slopes of Monte Maiella, of the sort in which we lived from 19–22 December

Thereupon we moved ourselves and our kit over to the second of the two huts, as it was farther away from the track and better hidden in the trees. We then set about preparing a meal; Scotty doing the cooking, Jack and Douglas collecting wood and I trying to cut up the meat. The only implement we had was a razor blade; so it was slow work and I cut my fingers about as much as I cut the meat.

We were all busy with these tasks when we heard a lot of shouting, and saw six Germans driving about twenty sheep through the woods. We debated whether to go off and hide in the woods, but decided it might look suspicious and give the game away. We had concocted a story if we were questioned. Scotty and I are students from Florence—my name is Jovani Giuseppi; Gillian is our sister and is married to Douglas. We are going to visit our sick parents at Archi, just the other side of the Sangro river. Jack works in Florence, but his home has been bombed.

A few minutes later we saw a mean looking German coming towards us with his rifle with bayonet fixed pointed at us. 'This is it,' we thought. I felt sick and angry that after all our efforts and the long journey, we should be arrested by this wretched little German. He came up and looked at us; we looked at him and then went on with what we were doing. He wandered round with his rifle at the ready pointing at us, while we tried to look unconcerned, though my heart was racing. Gillian then asked him in Italian what he wanted, but he made no reply. He probably could not understand Italian. He stood around for a while and was obviously puzzled. Presently he went away to call one of his colleagues over, and the two stood watching us from about twenty yards. We tried to give the impression we had ceased to notice them, and they wandered off a few minutes later.

Although we realised we were bound to encounter Germans as we were, if not exactly in their forward defensive positions, certainly in their gun lines; we did not want another scare like that. We decided it was too dangerous to stay in this hut. So next morning Jack and I took our kit down to near where we used to be, and hid it in the woods, while Scotty and Douglas went with Gillian to Rapino to try to get food. Jack and I then went to explore the Aquafreddo gorge looking for a cave we could move into. When near the end of the gorge we saw two Germans standing on a track about two hundred yards away. They shouted something unintelligible at us, and then began to come towards us. So Jack and I retraced our steps, trying to walk leisurely. After going a short way a shot rang out and a bullet whistled over our heads. More shouting from the Germans, so we quickened our pace; then another shot, much closer this time. Fortunately we reached the cover of some trees and soon put a good distance between ourselves and the Germans.

Scotty and Douglas returned having had no luck. We decided to move into a hut near the spring. It was similar to the one we were in yesterday, being made of pine trunks with a roof of pine needles matted together. As one end was open, we thought we would be able to have a fire of wood without being smoked out. Gillian returned from Rapino, where she had been told a grim story. About 6.30 p.m. the previous evening the Germans had entered the village, ordering everyone to leave their homes within half an hour, taking only the possessions they could carry. When the half hour was up, they hurried the people up by firing shots over their heads. The villagers having left, the Germans went round the houses helping themselves to anything they wanted. So it was obvious we were not going to be able to get any more food from there.

That evening we again discussed our situation. It was becoming plain that food supplies were gradually running out. Also the Germans were adopting a more aggressive policy to the people of the district. We had encountered them much more frequently these last few days. Accordingly we resolved to try to get through the lines on the night of 24th/25th December, hoping that the Germans might be celebrating

Christmas that night and be slightly less alert, unless an opportunity occurs before then. It was now 20th December.

The next day Douglas, Scotty and I set off across the Aquafreddo gorge to try to establish whether the track on the high ground on the other side led down to the Rapino to Penne Piedimonte road. The mist was as thick as ever. On the way we passed groups of shepherds and their families standing about disconsolately, their sheep having been stolen by the Germans. We followed the track downhill. After about three hundred yards we heard some Germans talking on our left, but we could not see them because the mist was so thick. This was one of their gun positions. Just to the right of the track where it joined the main road was another. We listened to them for a few minutes and then went back up the track. As we walked we became aware of a German Alpine soldier coming up the track about twenty yards behind us. We tried not to look as if we were hurrying and soon were able to swing off to the right on to some open ground.

Presently we came across more groups of shepherds sitting in front of small fires. When we asked them if we could buy some food, they all said 'No' as they had very little for themselves. But one man asked us to follow him to where four thin sheep were grazing. He caught one, killed it and gave it to us. We asked him how much he wanted for it, the proper price would have been about two hundred and fifty lira. But now his sheep had little value as the great majority had been stolen by the Germans. So we gave him thirty five lira which was all we had. The next problem was the skinning and gutting of it. We had no implement to do it, and would have made a mess of it anyway. The man would not do it, so we took the carcase across to the first group of shepherds. After some discussion one of these agreed to skin and gut it for us, which he did very quickly and efficiently. We carried the prepared sheep across a stick back to where Jack and Gillian were. They were most surprised, and there was much excitement between us that at least our meat supplies were safe for the present.

The food we missed most at that moment was bread. We hung the sheep in a hut a few yards away from the one in which we were living.

This hut stood back from a path and was partially concealed by trees. It was about twelve feet deep and ten feet wide. The walls were constructed of fir trunks three to four inches in diameter lashed together. The roof was made of fir branches intertwined and tied into the walls. The floor was fairly flat bare earth, hard to lie on. The stumps of the trees which went to make the hut stuck up an inch or two above the level of the floor and could be uncomfortable when lying down. However the whole thing was reasonably weather proof, though heavy rain dripped through. In any case in this prevailing mist everything was damp.

Later, Scotty and Gillian began to prepare the evening meal, while the rest of us collected water and wood. As we were doing this we noticed the sound of shelling seemed much closer than usual. We realised that the British gunners were firing airburst shells at the German Alpine soldiers' positions on the Maiella, and one of the shells burst quite close to Scotty.*

Douglas and I remarked how tired we were. I had noticed this especially during the last few days. We had no energy and going up the steep gradients was a big effort. I suppose it was because we were not getting enough food, or enough energising food. Certainly I had felt very hungry since we had come to the Maiella area. But this was the first time since leaving camp back in September that we had been short of food, so we could consider ourselves very fortunate. Despite prolonged boiling the meat was tough, and we still felt hungry when we had finished the meal. So we decided to have some porridge. I had been carrying in my sack two tins, saved from

---

* About a year later I happened to meet the Battery Commander of the 3.7" anti-aircraft artillery which had been doing the shooting that day.

Red Cross parcels. When it was cooked we handed it round and round between the five of us, each taking a spoon. It was warm and filling and we really enjoyed it.

Next morning, the 22nd December, after a cold sleepless night, we got up to find the sun shining with every prospect of a fine day. It is trite to say this lifted our spirits. A warm sunny day after bad weather always cheers one up. But it was particularly so on this occasion. We had been living almost continuously in thick dripping mist for nine days. Apart from this, a clear day meant there was a good chance we would be able to see the ground to the east and south east where the battle was being fought and get an idea of the respective German and British positions.

Leaving Scotty to look after the kit the rest of us went down to the spring to wash and shave. As we were doing this, a group of about twelve or fifteen Italians came up to fill their water bottles. Gillian and Douglas started talking to them. They had come from further north and were intending going through the line, which they did not think would be difficult in daylight. Douglas had the idea that we might go with them and perhaps get through in the crowd. We all agreed it would be worth the try.

Through the Lines

THE Italian party was made up of men varying from middle age to a boy of about seventeen, and one girl. They were keen to be off at once, but promised to wait for a few minutes while I fetched Scotty. I ran back to the hut and considerably surprised him with the statement: 'We are going to try to get through with a crowd of Italians, starting NOW.' He went to tell the English lads in their cave that we were going, and if we were not back by tomorrow night, they could have our sheep. I collected the things we wanted in our best sack; these were a tin of meat, a tin of biscuits, some Ovaltine tablets, Jack's shaving kit, my diary notes and my pullover. Unfortunately in our hurry to get away, Scotty left the list of next of kin addresses of the British soldiers we had met on our journey. We folded up the blanket and other kit and left them in the hut near the sheep, and off we went.

On reaching the spring we found the others had gone on. We half ran and half walked down to the stream and up the other side; catching up with the others at the place in the woods where we talked to the shepherds yesterday. Big deliberations were going on among the Italians, which held us up for at least a quarter of an hour. After some persuasion from us, we eventually moved on. Presently we reached the edge of the wood bordering the open grassy plateau. There was another halt, and it became obvious that the Italians' keenness to get through today, which they had shown earlier, had markedly cooled. So we sat down and watched the signs of battle.

In addition to the usual shelling, we watched three waves of Flying Fortresses come over and bomb Orsogna. Their targets were indicated by the artillery firing blue smoke. They were followed by a wave of Mitchell medium bombers attacking the same town. It was an amazing experience sitting on this high ground having a grandstand view of the battle and the most impressive fire support from the Allied Air Forces. The heavy bombers were followed by the fighter bombers diving down to attack enemy positions round Orsogna and further back towards Filetto and San Martino. When the bombing was finished, the artillery opened up with concentrations on Orsogna and along the ridge to Arielli. At the same time there was an explosion, causing an electric pylon on the low ground between Commino and Rapino to crash to the earth. Soon after another pylon was blown up, and it seemed that the Germans were destroying the electric cable line which ran towards the British positions. The Italian who seemed to be the leader of the party said: 'The Germans are withdrawing' and therefore it would be wiser to remain where we were. After talking round in circles for about half an hour without any decision being reached, we decided to push off on our own on a reconnaissance.

We crossed the piece of open ground which we now knew well and came to the track which Douglas, Scotty and I went down yesterday. But now we crossed it and climbed up a steep ridge into a wood. We had never been as far as this before, but having come so far we might as well go a bit farther. So we continued through the wood and came to the edge of an immense gorge called Garafano. It had steeper sides and looked deeper than the Aquafreddo. We debated whether to cross this and go on south towards Penne Piedimonte, or try to go down nearer Guardiagrele. I suggested we should cross the gorge and climb to the high ground which overlooked the road from Rapino to Penne Piedimonte. We set off to do this and were some way down the side of the gorge, when we saw a German camp near the bottom. There were a few tents well camouflaged with foliage, several mules and two or three Germans standing about. Reckoning we had not been seen, we watched them for a few minutes. It meant that we could not cross the Garafano gorge in daylight. Instead we returned to the top of the ridge, went along it in a north easterly direction to the edge of the wood, and out on to open flat ground which is called Bocca di Valle.

From this vantage point we had a very good view. To the north and north east we could see Pretoro and Rapino, and the roads and ridges running towards Chieti. More to the east was Orsogna, Guardiagrele and in the distance Lanciano and Ortona. Just north of the road running west from Guardiagrele, before it joins the Rapino to Penne Piedimonte road, was the small village of Commino. To the south east was the river Aventino, a tributary of the river Sangro, and the town of Casoli standing up on a promontory on the far bank. Running approximately north and south from the German positions towards the British was the Lajo stream.

The most interesting thing we saw from this point was the German guns firing, and being able to observe where their

Guardiagrele, standing up on its ridge, became a fortress in the German Gustav Line

shells landed, which was on a plateau called Piano di Laroma. Shells were also exploding on the high ground round San Domenico, south east of Guardiagrele. This indicated the position of the forward British troops. Piano di Laroma looked quite close. We spotted all the German gun positions, including the two where we had heard Germans talking yesterday.

As we were watching this great battle panorama below us, Jack said: 'I think we should try to go through tonight.' I agreed immediately. Jack, Scotty and I had often discussed big decisions between the three of us and sooner or later come to an agreement. Now there were five of us. I pointed out that this excellent view had given us a clear picture of the battle field and the whereabouts of the German and British positions. We would never get a better. We discussed it in detail and argued the pros and cons. Everyone gave his opinion. Gillian was keen to try. Scotty was undecided but would abide by the majority decision. Douglas was against it. He argued that this was only a reconnaissance and as we had previously agreed to go on the night of the 24th/25th December, we should stick to that. Jack and I pointed out there was no particular merit about the 24th, and now we had come so far and seen so much, we should take our chance and have a go. If nothing else, it would save us a walk back to our cave. Perhaps swayed by the fact that Gillian wanted to try, Douglas eventually agreed.

That being decided, we then had to plan how we were going to do it and which route we were going to take. We started to observe any signs of movement in the German lines. We looked for road blocks, sentry posts and routine transport movement. In fact we saw very little. One or two old and tired looking German trucks came up the road from Rapino and went out of our sight towards Penne Piedimonte. Most of them seemed to stop at a house on the roadside near the point where the track that Douglas, Scotty and I went down yesterday, joins the main road. Perhaps that was some sort of check point. A few civilians were wandering round

Commino, but there was no movement at Guardiagrele. Having more or less decided on our route, we got up and went towards the wood. Here we met a shepherd, and for confirmation we asked him the best route to take. He said several ex prisoners of war had gone through in the last few weeks, which was encouraging.

The route described by the shepherd as the best was, with one or two small exceptions, the one we had agreed among ourselves. We would go down this hillside till we join the track at about the point Scotty, Douglas and I reached yesterday; and follow it down, going very quietly past the two German gun positions, till it meets the Rapino to Penne Piedimonte road, cross it and go down the track towards Commino. Then we will strike off to the right, go through some olive groves, and up over terraced ground till we meet the road from Guardiagrele which joins the Rapino to Penne Piedimonte road. We cross this and travel east of south till we come down to the Lajo stream. Then we follow this down until it meets the river Aventino near Casoli. In the early stages of following this stream, we should see Guardiagrele and the outline of the ridge on which it stands, on our left. This should be a good guide.

We went back to the wood and opened our last tin of meat and biscuits, which came from Red Cross parcels and which Jack and I have been carrying since we left the camp. These made a very satisfactory meal. I think we all felt relieved we had come to a decision, and now we knew exactly what we had to do. All wonderings, doubts and waiting are behind us. We should either be successful or we should be recaptured—back 'in the bag' as we termed it. It never occurred to me that we would go so far, decide better of it and turn round and come back. My only worry was the possibility of stumbling on a post and being shot up or of walking on to a minefield.

We set off about 6.00 p.m., as it was getting dark. Having crossed some fields, we hit the track and went slowly and very carefully down it past the German gun positions on our left.

We seemed to be making a lot of noise, but we reached the road without incident. We crossed this walking normally, as any other method might have attracted suspicion. We then followed the track to Commino for about two hundred yards, over a wall to our right, across the garden of a house and over a small stream. The order was Jack leading, then Gillian, myself, Scotty and Douglas at the rear. As we climbed up towards the Guardiagrele-Penne Piedimonte road, we had to cross several fences and awkward walls and it was heavy going. But so far everything was going according to plan. However I noticed that Jack in his keenness to push on, was going straight on after each fence or wall and was getting too far ahead. I told him it was essential he wait at each obstacle to allow the others to catch up. So he said: 'All right you lead,' which I did. The night was intensely dark, even though our eyes had become accustomed to it. Scotty said afterwards it was the sort of darkness you could feel. We could see only about two yards in front of us. Our route lay up all the time and it seemed to take ages to reach the road. When eventually we got to it, we heard a horse and cart approaching. So we lay down to wait for it to pass. It was a German medium sized baggage wagon.

We crossed the road and continued to climb steadily. At this point we had a discussion as to whether to go straight on or swing to the left. We went straight on and presently came to the top of the ridge. The ground was uneven and the going very difficult. It was so dark we could hardly see where we were putting our feet. We passed two deserted houses. Then to our surprise we heard the noise of a truck approaching. It was a German half track going towards Penne Piedimonte. We now realised we had gone much too far to the right; we should not have been near this road. So we moved off to the left. After going for a little distance the ground began to fall away very steeply. This we thought was the approach to the Lajo stream.

With difficulty we clambered down this hillside and crossed a muddy bog, which I suppose was a small stream. We set to climb up the other side, but after about ten yards the gradient became almost vertical. The earth was thick, sticky mud, and we had to drag ourselves up by hands and knees. Eventually we hauled ourselves to the top. Then to our dismay we found there was a similar ravine in front of us. We tried to carry on down the ridge, but came to a place where it fell away almost vertically. So we were forced to try to go down into this ravine and up the other side. My left boot was now in such a bad state with the top very nearly off and the only thing between my foot and the soil was my sock, making it difficult to walk. Because of this Jack took the lead again.

We started to descend into the ravine and immediately we were in difficulties. The surface was loose and when one tried to get a foothold the earth fell away. The feeling of putting one's foot down and then sliding for several feet was most disconcerting. It took Jack and I about a quarter of an hour to descend about ten yards. We looked back and found the others were not following. They were having a frightful time further up. Gillian had got into a position where she could move neither forward nor back. This was not the sort of trip a girl should be on, but she was very determined and never complained. Jack and I managed to climb back up and help the others down to where we had reached. I suggested we might wait here till the moon came up at about 3.00 a.m., so we could see better. The intense darkness made the problem of negotiating these clay screes much more difficult. But our wish to get out of this frightful place overrode everything else, including the possibility of running into Germans. So we decided to struggle on.

As we went down the loose earth gave way to sticky mud. Another twenty minutes scrambling and sliding down brought us to the bottom. Here the mud was so soft we sank in over our ankles. Having made several attempts to cross, we at last found a place which was slightly less soft. Once across we kept

ASSISTED PASSAGE

to the bottom of the ravine, looking for a good place to climb up out of it again. We could only pray there were no more of these ravines to cross. After going about a hundred and fifty yards down, we came to a spot where the sides of the ravine did not seem so steep. Scotty found a signal cable here. We started to climb again, but about half way up Jack got stuck. I managed to find another way and then hauled him up. It was a matter of going a yard or two, then hauling up the person behind you, then staggering for another yard or two.

After what seemed an interminable time we reached the top, and to our immense relief we saw a field in front of us. We thanked God we were out of that frightful ravine. We estimated we had taken two hours to cover what could not have been more than five hundred yards. Mud was now caked all down the front of our clothes.

We sat down for a rest at the edge of the field, and I produced the tin of Ovaltine tablets, also saved from a Red Cross parcel. The night was now not quite so dark, as the stars which previously had been screened by low cloud, could now be seen. Our guide for direction was now the Lajo valley, which was fairly easy to follow. Just after we set off again we heard voices, which Gillian recognised as German, about thirty yards away on our right. So we moved very slowly and as quietly as we could, which was not easy as the wet and sticky soil clung to one's boots. The way led over cultivated fields, past one or two deserted farmhouses and through vines supported on posts. As we walked, the dark shape of Guardiagrele and the ridge on which it stood loomed up on our left. It seemed very close, but was in fact nearly one and a quarter miles from us. Then we saw tracer bullets being fired from the ridge towards the Lajo valley, and soon after the crackle of a machine gun. Fortunately the bullets were well away from us.

We were now making better progress, though the going was still fairly slow. We knew we just had to follow the Lajo valley and it would lead us in the right direction. We kept about two hundred yards to the right of it. The fields were undulating and it was up and down little ridges all the way. The gullies were standing in water as small streams ran into the Lajo.

About an hour after we left the clay screes, we came to another very large ravine, more rocky than the others and seemingly very deep. The shepherd had mentioned this yesterday evening. Jack thought the best way was to go round to the head of it to the right. The rest of us favoured going left to where the stream joins the Lajo. However we did turn right and went up the edge of the ravine for several hundred yards, but there was no sign of the end of it. So we retraced our steps and went downhill to the point where the gorge ran out into the valley of the Lajo.

Just before we reached this Jack, who was in front, lay down; I immediately did the same. There were two men, carrying what looked like sub-machine guns, under the trees near the stream. Gillian, Scotty and Douglas closed up with Jack and I, and we signalled them to get down. They seemed to make a frightful noise as they lifted their feet from the sticky mud. We lay there for fully a quarter of an hour looking at this patrol, and they looked at us. I thought I could make out a German helmet on the head of one man. I comforted myself with the thought that perhaps they were as nervous as we were. Then they moved and they made as much noise as we had done, it being almost impossible to move silently with the ground conditions as they were. The enemy patrol (I say enemy because both Jack and I thought they were Germans) began to move off into the trees, so after a few minutes we slid down the bank to the stream which we crossed very cautiously, and up the other side and out of sight. Scotty and Douglas then asked what all the excitement was about! They had not seen the patrol.

We continued walking on our previous line about two hundred yards to the right of the Lajo stream, up and down little ridges with wet gullies in the bottom, but none difficult to cross. We seemed to have been walking for ages and Gillian, and indeed the rest of us, were getting very tired. So we stopped for frequent short rests, when my Ovaltine tablets were passed round. We had not expected the journey would be so long and were beginning to wonder when it would end. These stops were never for more than a few minutes, as we soon got cold standing about.

After walking for another hour or more we came to three or four houses which made up a big farm. They seemed to be undamaged and one looked as if it might be inhabited. Thinking we might be approaching our lines, we looked up to the right to see if we could see the plateau, Piano di Laroma, which from our observations yesterday, we thought was occupied by the British. Several times we thought we saw it, but it was only a small ridge we were looking at. About 4.15 a.m. the moon, which was in its last quarter, was beginning to rise. Then we definitely did see the plateau. That meant we did not have far to go.

We passed through three small woods and over some awkward fences. Then we heard spasmodic British shelling, and the sounds of the guns seemed to be coming from behind us. That was another good sign. Next we struck a rough secondary road which we knew must lead in the direction of Casoli. After walking on this for about half a mile, we came to some houses where several jeeps towing small 75 mm guns, motor cycles and one or two trucks were parked. This was certainly British equipment. Then a man stepped out of a doorway and shouted 'Halt, who goes there?' We hastened to reply 'Friend.' He then said 'Give the password.' I remember thinking how nice it was to hear a free British soldier's voice again. Scotty and I explained we were British officers who had been prisoners of war, and therefore we could not know the password. The sentry came up and looked at us very closely with a puzzled expression on his face. Without demanding any proof in the form of identity cards or the like, he showed us into the Guard Room. It was nearly 5.00 a.m.

The fact that we were 'through the line,' and among free men once more, was only now fully brought home to us. All the same our emotions were subdued, as perhaps might be expected among a group of English people. We did not embrace or clap each other on the back. I was filled with immense thankfulness and relief that we had completed the long journey safely, with a certain satisfaction that we had been successful.

Our arrival in the Guard Room caused quite a commotion. The men got up from improvised beds and made room for us. Lukewarm tea, biscuits and margarine were produced. Everyone including ourselves started asking questions. We had come into an artillery troop headquarters of the 1st Airborne Division which was holding positions on the left of the 8th Army front. They told us that 50 Division had been sent home after the end of the Sicilian campaign. This was good news, as it meant we could rejoin them in England. After 'stand to' at 6.00 a.m. breakfast of bacon, sausage, biscuits and tea was produced. This was most welcome as we were very hungry.

A little later we were taken in two jeeps back to the Battery and Regimental headquarters of the artillery. We gave the Battery commander all the information we could on the layout of the German defences and marked on his map the positions of the enemy artillery near Commino and Rapino. We were then taken to Brigade headquarters as we had been told the Brigade commander wanted to see us. I felt nervous about this because we were not fit to be seen by any brigadier. Both Scotty's and my trousers were badly torn, my boots were flapping on my feet and were absolutely finished, and Douglas's jacket had gaping holes. Also our clothes were covered in caked mud from the clay screes we had climbed the previous night. However the brigadier was very nice, congratulating us and asked which way we had come. Both he and us were surprised that the first troops we had encountered was a Royal Artillery troop headquarters. I felt awkward and rather ashamed as I talked to him, because I could not resist constantly scratching as my skin was so irritable from the lice infestation.

From Brigade headquarters we were driven to Atessa where 13 Corps Field Maintenance Centre was situated. On the journey I was amazed at the quantity of vehicles and equipment to be seen everywhere, in marked contrast to the situation behind the German lines, where one saw only an occasional truck, some of them horse drawn, and a few motor cycles. Approaching Atessa, I looked back at the snow capped Maiella range standing up bold and forbidding, with steep ridges running from it towards the coast. It was on those ridges we had lived for nine days right in the German forward area. It made one realise what a difficult country Italy is to fight in, particular in winter.

On arrival at Atessa we were taken to the Town Major's office. He was surprised and perhaps a little shocked to see such scarecrows walk into his office. But he said he would fit us out with a full issue of personal clothing—battle dress, shirt, underclothes, socks, towel and shaving kit. We all gave our particulars to his clerk, and then asked if we could have a bath. A lieutenant in the Royal Corps of Signals volunteered that we could have one in his billet, where he filled two big tubs with hot water. This was the first hot bath we had had since leaving the camp on 8th September and the first of any sort since 1st December. It was one of the most pleasurable physical experiences of my life. We scrubbed the weeks of accumulated dirt from our bodies, and made sure we got rid of the lice. Our Italian clothes were taken outside and burnt.

While we were bathing and dressing a captain in the Intelligence Corps came to talk to us. We told him our story and gave him as much information as we could. Our situation was straightforward, but he was concerned about Gillian, much to Douglas's annoyance. He had to make certain she was a genuine refugee and not something more sinister. We dressed in our new issue clothing and Gillian looked rather peculiar attired in British battle dress. We soon felt too hot.

The contrast in warmth from our thin Italian clothes was enormous. It was not long before I discarded the vest. However we got used to the extra warmth in a day or two.

Having been told we were too late to catch the transport for Termoli which was the railhead, we decided to spend Christmas at Atessa, where we were well looked after and entertained by the officers who lived at the Field Maintenance Centre mess. After Christmas we passed into the hands of the organisation which had been set up to handle ex-prisoners of war. They had expected many thousands, (there were approximately fifty thousand British prisoners in Italy at the Armistice), but so far only about five thousand had come through. We moved through Termoli to Bari, and sailed from there on the afternoon of 31st December 1943 bound for Algiers.

I reflected how lucky or fortunate we had been. So many times we might have gone another way or arrived at a different time, and run into Germans. The German inability to distinguish us from Italians had saved us on more than one occasion, especially during the last nine days when we were in 'the shadow of the Maiella'. Whereas the Italians knew instantly we were not one of them. Nor did we fall seriously ill or have a bad accident.

Perhaps a measure of our luck, if one wants to call it that, was the estimate of Tony Davies in his book *When the Moon Rises* that of the five hundred or so officers and men who marched out of Campo PG 49 on 9th September 1943, 'only a tenth succeeded in reaching the Allied lines, or even remaining free for very long'.

Hence my firm belief that we were guided by the hand of God.

ASSISTED PASSAGE

Epilogue

ON New Year's Eve we sailed through an enormous storm. I reckoned I was better staying on deck, and managed not to be seasick. On the ship were a number of small groups and mixed details including sailors who had been on destroyers and corvettes in the Atlantic. Some of them were very seasick. This gave me the false impression that I was a good sailor. I learnt differently when we were sailing for Normandy on D Day. We heard next morning that the ship, which was designed for service only in the Mediterranean, was rolling so much it nearly went beyond the danger point.

After a month in Algiers waiting for a convoy we sailed for England on the 8th February 1944, arriving in Liverpool the next day. We were given two months leave on double rations, and before the end I was putting on more weight than was good for me.

I had always wanted to get back to 8 D.L.I. where most of my friends were, with several of whom I had been since the beginning of the war. So, much to my parents' disappointment and anxiety, I managed to pull strings to obtain the posting I wanted. I rejoined 8 D.L.I. as a company commander on the 28th April 1944. 8 D.L.I. was still one of three Durham battalions in 151 Brigade of 50 Division. This was one of the divisions which had been brought home from the Mediterranean to lead the assault on the Normandy beaches on the 6th June. I was with them until being wounded on the 12th September at Gheel in Belgium.

Jack Moore saw it as his duty to rejoin his old unit, the Northumberland Hussars Anti-Tank Regiment, and in spite of his wife's entreaties, sailed with them to France. To be killed by enemy action would not be unexpected. But Jack was killed in a road accident in Normandy; a gross waste of a fine officer and a tragic loss.

Scotty White married his fiancée on his return to England. He continued to serve, but not abroad, until the end of the war.

Sadly we lost touch with both Douglas De Cent and Gillian Weatherall and I have no idea how they fared for the rest of the war. There was a note in a national newspaper (probably the *Daily Telegraph*) in January or February 1956 that Gillian Gensini described as 'a charming and resourceful English woman who escaped from an Italian prison camp in 1943, and later worked in the Foreign Office,' was in charge of a National Union of Students Flag Day on the 25th February 1956 to raise funds for a new hostel in central London. Sadly, I know no more than that.

Postscript September 1992

IN order to try to get some photographs for this book, my wife, daughter and I flew to Italy in September 1992. It was my first visit since 1943.

Obviously so much has changed. The roads are wider, better and carrying vastly more traffic than in 1943, but in the country and hill areas they are just as twisty and have as many hairpin bends as ever. Many of the routes we remembered as tracks are now roads. Many new houses have been built. The country people are more prosperous and better dressed. Indeed it would be a very bad state of affairs if their life style had not markedly improved during the last half century.

Nevertheless many things were unchanged, and I was surprised how easy it was to recognise most of the places we visited, after a gap of forty nine years.

The *Orfanotrofio* at Fontanellato, the site of Campo PG 49, was instantly recognisable. It is now unoccupied and has an air of creeping dereliction. The parade ground at the back of the building is just the same, but the trees on the east and west sides have grown large and tall, which gives a much more closed-in atmosphere. The playing field is now a public park. An impressive plaque has been placed at the main gate. The inscription states:—

> This plaque records the fortieth Anniversary of the imprisonment of English and Allied prisoners of war who were interned in Campo Concentramento PG 49. The people of Fontanellato who after the Armistice on the 8th September 1943, helped them and hid them at the risk of severe repercussions.
> Fontanellato 11 September 1983.

Poggio Cancelli has a more benign and prosperous look. We saw it at its worst in 1943 when it was covered in snow. There is much new building, but I could recognise the houses we had been in, though they have been greatly improved in the intervening years. San Stefano and Calascio seemed just the same. Having seen it on a warm sunny day last September, I cannot now imagine how we managed the long climb up the bare hill in the gathering dusk to Rocca Calascio on the 20th November 1943.

The country round Colle and Corvara north of the river Pescara is not quite as I remember it. The hills are steeper, the farms fewer and with better buildings. Corvara looked even more as if it has grown out of the bare precipitous rock on which it stands.

The dam and the sluice gates over which we crossed the Pescara river are just the same and I recognised it immediately. The area in which we lived for nine days 'in the shadow of the Maiella' is now covered by a dense forest of fir trees. Many are probably the same trees that we saw, but are now so high and thick that I could not find exactly where we had been. The track at Bocca di Valle leading down past the German positions to the point where it joined the Rapino to Penne Piedimonte road is itself a fine road now. I could easily follow the route we took when we were going through the lines. There is now a new road from Guardiagrele to Casoli running first east of and later crossing the Lajo stream at about half way to Casoli. The clay screes look as formidable as they were in December 1943. The route we followed about two hundred yards to the west of the Lajo stream is more undulating than I remembered it. We had good cause to be tired by the time we reached the British post.

The country people, *contadini* if that is the right term nowadays, are as jolly, friendly and helpful as ever. Unfortunately we could not get close to them because of our

POSTSCRIPT

inability to speak more than a few words of Italian. I do not doubt that if the circumstances occurred again, these people would act in the same way as their parents or grandparents did in 1943.

ASSISTED PASSAGE

IAN ENGLISH was born in Co. Durham and educated at Oundle School where he was Head Boy in his last term. He was commissioned into the Territorial Army in 1938, joining 8th Battalion the Durham Light Infantry. He served with them in the BEF Campaign in 1940. In the Gazala battles in the Desert he was awarded the Military Cross, and was involved in the fighting at El Alamein, where he gained a Bar to the MC. He was taken prisoner at the end of the Battle of Mareth in March 1943.

After leaving Italy, Ian English returned to UK and rejoined 8 DLI in time for the D Day Landings and the fighting in Normandy where he won a second Bar to the MC, one of only 24 to gain this distinction in World War II. At the end of the war he was Second in Command of his battalion.

On demobilisation he went up to Cambridge University where he gained a Degree in Agriculture. He then joined Fisons Limited as an Agricultural Adviser and was with them for 30 years. Now retired, he and his Danish wife live in Wensleydale. His hobbies are bird watching, gardening and military history.

He is co-author of *Into Battle with the Durhams*, the history of 8 DLI in Wold War II.